Through the worst financial crisis of the last seventy years, North Dakota hardly hiccupped. They've now had the lowest unemployment rate in the nation for four years running. Add to that a foreclosure rate half that of almost any other state in the country.

What's with North Dakota?

Anonymous kindness, says Marc de Celle: "The oil boom on the western side of North Dakota helps, for sure – but here on the eastern side of the state, the Fargo side, it's a much more remarkable story – a story of bankers quietly refusing, during the crazy years at the beginning of the 21st Century, to sell the profitable mortgages that bankers and brokers across the rest of the United States were going nuts over. Why? Because around here, people don't like selling things that don't make good sense or, worse yet, things that might hurt people.

"Even if they're profitable. Even if they're bankers.

"So while the rest of the United States has experienced the worst financial crisis in seventy years as a result of the subprime mortgage mess," he says, "North Dakota never had a mess, or a crisis."

In this deceptively simple, funny, heartwarming book, filled with de Celle's stories from his family's first five years in Fargo, he makes a surprisingly convincing case for what he calls "Northern Prairie Culture." Because de Celle has a secret he keeps for most of the book. He's not just a good storyteller. He's also a compulsive researcher.

You may think, at first, you're just reading laugh-till-you-cry stories about the over-the-top generosity and kindness of the Northern Prairie folks populating these pages. But by the time you've read through *Notes on the Chapters* at the end, you might find yourself with a different view of humanity, and our possibilities, than you previously thought possible.

"*How Fargo of You* is heartwarming and *hilarious.* I found extreme delight in Marc de Celle's newcomer observations of what most of us take for granted in this part of the country. It's a great read." — **Dennis Walaker, Mayor of Fargo**

"I *love* this book. Five minutes into de Celle's astounding journey into Fargoism, I was having trouble believing the place he was describing really existed. I fell in love with it anyway. By the last page, I knew Northern Prairie Culture was real, glad for it, and grateful a writer of de Celle's caliber gave me the tour." — **David Madrid, a journalist who works for *The Arizona Republic* and the creator of *fabulousfables.com***

"It took an outsider coming in to finally capture the essence of Fargo. If you live within a few hundred miles of here and are tired of people in other parts of the country wondering why, *send them this book.*" — **Adrienne Olson, Director of Communications and Community Relations, Fargo Moorhead West Fargo Chamber of Commerce**

"*How Fargo of You* will make you laugh out loud with tears in your eyes! I just read the book and loved it. Marc de Celle is a wonderful ambassador for our cold winters and warm hearts. He gives the world an inside view of Northern Prairie Culture seldom seen by outsiders, while reminding those of us who call Fargo home why we're so lucky to live here." — **Kerstin Kealy, Anchor, WDAY6 TV, Fargo**

How Fargo of You

Stories from the Northern Prairie
That People Who Haven't Been Here
Will Never Believe

How Fargo of You
Stories from the Northern Prairie
That People Who Haven't Been Here
Will Never Believe

Fargo Crossing™

How Fargo of You™
www.howfargo.com
Third Edition, November 2011
Printed in Fargo by Forum Communications Printing
ISBN 978-0-9830928-0-3

To Charlene and Melody,
without whom I would never
have discovered Fargo,

Anastasia and Austen,
without whom we never
would have moved here,

Dennis and most of the
teenagers within a hundred miles,
without whom Fargo would be
another disaster area,

and Joan, without whom
How Fargo of You
might never have
been written.

Contents

Learning to Speak Fargo

It's not bizarre. It's brilliant.

It was early December, 2010. The First Edition of *How Fargo of You* had just been released.

"Hi, caller, what's your name?" I was sitting across from Dan Michaels, morning DJ for the *Eagle* radio station in Fargo. He'd just asked people to call in with their own *How Fargo of You* stories, and the switchboard had lit up like a Christmas tree.

"Well, my name's Lou, and I just got into town last week, and I had my first *How Fargo of You* experience the night I got into town."

"What happened, Lou?" Dan asked in his big, friendly voice.

"Well, I've never driven in snow before..."

"Oooooh," I cringed involuntarily, and all three of us started laughing. I looked at Dan. "I gotta hear this."

"Yeah, well," Lou continued, still chuckling, "so as soon as I got into town I got stuck in a snow bank on Broadway..."

More laughter all around. By now, I could detect that Lou had some kind of southern accent.

"So then what happened, Lou?" Dan was smiling at me. We both had an idea of what was coming. But we were about to find out it was even better.

"Well, it was about seven at night, it was already dark out, and I wasn't sure what to do. The nearest thing I saw open was a bar called the Bismarck..."

Dan and I again erupted in laughter. It was alright. Lou was chuckling, too. The Bismarck, at the north end of downtown Fargo, is, well, just about the most Viking bar on the North American Continent in the 21st Century, I'd guess.

"So I went in," Lou continued, "and I gotta tell you, I'm a black guy from Louisiana, so I wasn't sure what to expect..."

Dan and I glanced at each other.

"...and I suddenly found myself surrounded by giant, bearded Norsemen..."

Dan and I lost it.

"So what happened then?" Dan asked as soon as he was able to speak again.

"Well, I kind of quietly walked up to the bar," Lou said, "and I asked the bartender if he had a phone I could use, and he said sure, and pointed to the end of the bar where there was a phone. But then one of the big guys at the bar asked why I needed a phone, so I told him what had happened, and he started to pull his cell phone out of his pocket, but while I was explaining he put it back in. Then *he pulled out his car keys and handed them to me!* And he said... *he said, 'Well, you can use my truck to get it out, it's got a strap in the back. It's the big red one parked right out front.'*"

"Whoa!" I let out. "Now **that's** a *How Fargo of You* story!"

"Yeah, where I come from people don't just hand their car keys to strangers!" Lou was kind of yelling now, still clearly amazed. "But I had no idea what to do, I mean, I've seen a couple people get pulled out of the snow since I got here so now I know what a strap is, and people carry them around to rescue each other. But when he held out his truck keys, I didn't take 'em. I mean, I was kinda stunned."

"I know what you mean, Lou," I said, "A lot of people like you and I who didn't grow up around here are sort of in a state of shock after our first Fargo, uh, our first few Fargo experiences."

"So then what happened, Lou?" Dan asked.

"Well, then, one of the other bearded giants elbowed the guy with the keys and said, 'Don't make him pull his own car out!' And all of a sudden there were three big guys walking out the door asking where my car was. And they didn't need a truck or a strap or anything. They just pushed me out of the snow bank I was buried in like it was nothing, you know, like three muscled-up young Santas."

"Well, Lou," Dan said through the laughter, "Welcome to Fargo!"

*   *   *

Lou was beginning to learn the language of Fargo. The *real* Fargo. When people first arrive in the Northern Prairie, they often expect folks to sound like the bizarre cartoon-like characters in the 1995 Coen brothers' movie *Fargo*. But what they find is very different. It's spoken without much of an accent, if any. Sometimes without any words at all.

It's the language of anonymous kindness.

A purse, accidentally dropped in a snowy parking lot, taken in to a restaurant manager who looks at the ID in the wallet and calls the lady who's lost it before she even realizes it's missing; everything inside is otherwise untouched, of course... A mother, buying her daughter a matching jacket and tights at Herberger's Department Store, discovers at the register, to her daughter's quiet disappointment, that she doesn't have enough money for the tights... and then, suddenly, the lady in line behind them insists on buying the tights for the girl: "They just go with the jacket so perfectly!"... The keys to a car are lent to a stranger – *an unknown teenager!* – in a coffee shop, by a person eating there who overheard him telling his mom on the phone that his car just broke down on his way to a prom fifty miles away, so he won't be able to make it and needs a ride home (her car, she told me, was a "beater that couldn't make the long trip" while dad was twenty miles away in Fargo with their good car, working late)... the teenager was simply asked to return the car to the coffee shop parking lot at the end of the night, tank refilled...

*   *   *

After the First Edition of *How Fargo of You* came out, I started hearing stories like these – from people I didn't know who'd just recognized me on the streets of Fargo – several times a day. What amazed me most was that almost all the incidents people were relating had just taken place in the last week or so! I wasn't hearing, for the most part, stories from the distant past. I was hearing about anonymous acts of kindness that had happened to people recently – just the latest iteration of Fargo they'd experienced.

This shouldn't have surprised me, I realized, when I later did the math. I could count at least thirty amazing gestures like these I'd personally been at the receiving end of during the five years I'd lived here before *How Fargo of You* was published. That's six a year. And there was no reason for anyone to take any special notice of me at that time. If all 200,000 people in the Fargo metro area are at the receiving end of six *How Fargo of You* stories every year, that adds up to way over a million amazing annual acts of kindness! Divided by 365 days a year, this would mean that something like three thousand such incidents, on average, occur every day within about a ten- or twenty-mile radius of downtown Fargo.

*   *   *

"OK," I can hear someone from New York or L.A. or somewhere else like I used to live saying, "That and five bucks'll get me a ham sandwich and…?"

Well, try 3.5 percent unemployment when the rest of the country is over 9 percent.[1] No, I'm not kidding – lowest in the nation. And there's a direct relationship between those numbers and the way people treat each other around here. The oil boom on the western side of North Dakota helps, for sure – but here on the eastern side of the state, it's a much more remarkable story – a story of bankers quietly refusing, during the crazy years at the

---

[1] See *Notes on the Chapters* at the end of the book for sources and details on these statistics and all others in the book.

beginning of the 21st Century, to sell the profitable mortgages that bankers and brokers across the rest of the United States were going nuts over. Why? Because around here, people don't like to sell things that might hurt people. Even if they're profitable. Even if they're bankers.

So while the rest of the United States has experienced the worst financial crisis in seventy years as a result of the subprime mortgage mess, we never had a mess, or a crisis. We have far and away the lowest foreclosure rate in the country, which you can read all about in Chapter 13, *How Lucky We Are*.

And along with your ham sandwich and rock-bottom unemployment and foreclosure rates, you'll also get the second highest high-school graduation rate in the country, and the second-highest number of people with two-year college degrees or better. Not that there's piles of money for fancy schools in everyone's pockets. Far from it. Simply put, good education is what happens when kids grow up in a healthy, nurturing, sane environment. But don't let me mislead you – those numbers don't even begin to describe what teenagers are like around here. You'll have to read through Chapter Two to get a glimpse of that remarkable reality.

Finally, along with your ham sandwich, rock-bottom unemployment and soaring education levels, you get crime rates at or near the lowest not just in our country, but the world. Because people here value people, relationships and community over stuff, money and power.

Learning to speak the language of Fargo has taught me many things these last few years, in one stunning encounter after another. But that last is probably the most important: Valuing stuff, money and power over people, relationships and community isn't okay – it's the orientation of a criminal. So when a culture begins to go that way, there goes that culture. But when a culture has those values on right, it's absolute magic.

In some ways, it's like a little piece of Heaven on Earth. I mean it. Before I came to Fargo, I didn't know this kind of place was humanly possible. I hadn't found a hint of it in Plato, Adam Smith, or Paine. In fact, Fargo has proven to me that human beings can behave a lot more deeply than anything any pages I've ever read dared to suggest.

But don't come running. Living here – *surviving* here – demands its fair share of sacrifice. If you're already seriously thinking of coming as you read this, quickly skip ahead to the Postscript at the end of the book, *Twelve Reasons to Come to Fargo, Twice as Many Not to.*

*   *   *

Contrary to the impression left by our celluloid namesake, there's nothing bizarre about speaking Fargo. I hope the pages between here and the Postscript – containing just a few of the more remarkable stories of how I learned to speak Fargo – illustrate this. These pages are my way of trying to pass a little bit of this remarkable language on to people who've never had the benefit of hearing it for themselves.

It's a *brilliant* language. Our country, and the world, desperately need to hear it – if only just a little, which is all I have to offer.

If **How Fargo of You** becomes a bestseller beyond Fargo, I'll take about one percent of the credit. Maybe two. These are really Fargo's stories, in Fargo's language. I just had the privilege of being at the receiving end.

There's just one thing to say to all the folks around here.

How Fargo of You.

Marc de Celle
November 1, 2011

How Fargo of You

How Fargo of You Stories

No dumb criminals with goofy accents.

I had no burning desire to visit Fargo. But my wife, Charlene, had decided we were going. Her best friend Melody, who I liked very much and our kids adored, now lived in Fargo. So we came. It was the summer of 2001 and we were on vacation.

Our lives would never be the same.

Until then, all I knew of Fargo, other than the fact that my wife's best friend had moved here, was that a movie with dumb

3

criminals talking in goofy accents had been titled after it. Oh, and it got really, *really* cold. Back in the '70s, living in L.A., I had a singer-songwriter friend named Skip who somehow ended up with a gig in Fargo during the Christmas holidays. He played the same venue several years running, returning to California every year with new tales of frozen woe.

"...It was only fifty feet from the front door of my hotel to the gig, but when I opened it, a twenty-below arctic blast hit me so hard I gasped... *sucking in the tundra!* My windpipe instantly *freeze-dried!* I staggered down the sidewalk, eyelashes freezing shut, trying not to slip on the ice, which probably would have broke my butt clean in two, because the ice up there is *hard*. I almost froze in place on the sidewalk and *died a frozen death*, but some guys in parkas saw me, opened the door to the bar and slid me inside. I stood there defrosting for a while. At first, I couldn't even shiver. I was a *frozen Skippy pop*.

"The owner saw me and started laughing. Said it was time for my first set. I started shuffling toward the stage, 'cause I couldn't pick my feet up off the floor. Then my body started shaking. I trembled my guitar out of its case and tried to play some simple three-chord song, but I was shaking so bad *it sounded like I had the reverb on*. Then I opened my mouth and heard something that sounded like Clint Eastwood trying to croak out tunes in *Paint Your Wagon*. Luckily, there was a nurse dressed up like a cocktail waitress roaming around who looked over as soon as she heard me, went behind the bar and brought over a weird looking bottle. Laughed and told me it was the stuff they use to *de-ice the wings of planes*. Said *they use that stuff for everything up there*. Applied it directly to my vocal chords *with a swizzle stick!* I remember my throat loosening up a little, but after that everything starts gettin' kinda fuzzy..."

Listening to Skip's highly creative rants about Fargo's colder moments, sitting on a balcony sipping margaritas on a balmy January evening in southern California – Skip's favorite "defrosting therapy" for at least two months after returning from Fargo – my stomach soon ached from laughter. And I became frightened. *Very* frightened. I vowed to stay as far south of North Dakota as possible. *Forever*.

That was all I knew of Fargo.

So our first visit, nearly a quarter of a century later, held many pleasant surprises. No dumb criminals – in fact, about the lowest crime rate in the country. No goofy accents, don'cha know. Great weather (we came in June). And a much bigger surprise, as you'll read in Chapter One, where I describe my first *How Fargo of You* story.

What's a *How Fargo of You* story? Well...

What should you say to the carpenter
you just met after he spends three hours doing a
great job putting a doggie door in your new house, but
then insists, "It's a housewarming gift," happily
rebuffing all attempts to pay him?

How Fargo of You.

What do you say when a neighbor
from a couple of houses down – a man you've
never met before, because you just moved to North
Dakota a few months ago – notices your wife stuck in the
snow on your long driveway, comes over and pushes her
out, then drives his big snow blower over and clears
the entire length of your driveway, wearing a big,
friendly smile the whole time?

How Fargo of You.

What do you say when you learn the
murder rate in Fargo is only *one-fiftieth* that of the
major metropolitan area you just moved away from,
while North Dakota's high school graduation rate
is the second highest in the country?

How Fargo of You.

What do you whisper to the couple
who are long gone – and who you've never
met – when the waitress tells you they already
paid for the great home-style meals you
and your son just finished eating?

How Fargo of You.

What do you think of your fellow drivers
as the freeway begins narrowing for a construction
zone and, despite ample opportunity for any of a hundred
drivers to pull a half-mile ahead and cut in, not one car
sails by during the three minutes it takes before the
orange cones narrow to a single lane?

How Fargo of You.

What do you yell out the window of your
van when you find yourself in the same construction
zone a month later and realize you've absent-mindedly done
what no one else around here is rude enough to do — you've
embarrassingly driven down the right lane as far as you can and
must now cut in… and when you muster the courage to look
over, not only is no one scowling at you, but the man in the
truck next to you is smiling and waving you ahead?

How Fargo of You!

What do you laughingly say to your radio
when you happen upon an important political debate
and it's so friendly and issue-oriented you can't tell which
of the two well-informed candidates is a Democrat
and which is a Republican?

How Fargo of You.

What do you say to your cab driver
when you learn that less than a year ago he was pulling
down close to six figures in a major American city, but he and
his wife decided he should quit his job so they could move back
to Fargo, where their two small children would be able
to grow up in a safe, friendly environment?

How Fargo of You.

What do you think when you learn
about demographic studies showing thousands
of local college graduates are like your cab driver – they move
to a major metropolis to accept a high-paying job, only to return
to Fargo when they start their families, so they can provide their
children with the same wholesome environment they
enjoyed while they were growing up?

How Fargo of You.

What do you say about the local
workforce when a former mayor tells you
he once worked with Cargill, the largest privately
held corporation in the country, to staff an accounting
office in Fargo intended to employ two hundred people… but
they stopped hiring after only about a hundred, because, they
told him, the workload that would normally keep a couple
hundred people busy in other places was already
getting done just fine by about half that
number in Fargo?

How Fargo of You.

What do you say when an executive
with the largest advertising, PR and communications firm between Minneapolis and Denver – a
Fargo company that's been around more than 60 years,
longer than 99 percent of the advertising agencies in the
world – gives you nine months of consulting and coaching
while you write your first full-fledged book and prepare
to promote it, but not one word is ever said about
money, despite your repeated efforts
to bring it up?

How Fargo of You.

What do you say when, due to a
dramatic change in the forecast for the
spring crest of the Red River, the mayor says
we only have about a week to produce two million
sandbags – and by the next day there are over 10,000
well-organized volunteers, about half in their teens,
some from hundreds of miles away, working all
across the city to get the sandbags made and
in place – and soon, the mayor's goals
are exceeded by more than a
million sandbags?

How Fargo of You.

What do you yell at the TV
when the Federal Government recommends
Fargo be evacuated to avoid flood danger, and in
response the mayor holds a press conference, saying no
able-bodied adult Fargoan need leave, because thousands
of these volunteer heroes are the only reason the town's
not already ten feet underwater – thereby saving
the city from a certain and severe
watery catastrophe?

How Fargo of You!

Those are just brief glimpses into a few of my many *How Fargo of You* stories – each one an episode I would have found completely unimaginable during the 45 years I spent living in California, Arizona and Florida before our first visit here nine years ago.

How Fargo of You stories happen all the time around here. If you've never visited the Northern Prairie, I should probably tell you: *I'm not kidding. All the time.* I had two more happen to me last week. I'll tell you the one that happened just last Friday afternoon.

I took a dog of ours, Geena (my daughter named her when she was just four years old) to the vet. Geena's an eighty-pound golden-colored Collie-Husky mix. She had a sore that wasn't healing.

Don't get the wrong idea. I'm not a frequent flyer when it comes to the vet. Some pet owners help their veterinarians afford a lake home with a high-tech fishing boat. Not me. I've even been known to let our dogs' vaccines lapse once in a while, so when it's time to renew their licenses or get their annual professional grooming I first have to take them in to get their shots updated. The point being, what you're about to read didn't happen because our pets are great customers over at the vet's place. Quite the opposite.

Anyway, Geena had no ordinary-looking sore. It was a weird little growth on the side of her neck that we'd never noticed until an amateur groomer (our normal groomer was on vacation) accidentally cut the top half of it off. (Yes, we pet

Geena all the time, but she has a virtual lion's mane around her neck, so we'd never noticed this weird little thing until the grooming injury.) Anyway, it wasn't healing, so my wife and kids started haranguing me. And that's how, last Friday, Geena and I ended up in one of the sterilized little pet patient rooms at the Airport Animal Hospital (it's by the airport).

After Geena and I had waited a minute or two in the clean little pet patient room, in walked Dr. Harvey. He's a tall, gentle, soft-spoken, friendly professional – like a lot of folks you'll meet in these pages. Geena showed him her sore and I explained its brief history. He started cleaning it off and explained it was a sebaceous something-or-other.

"These are common in older dogs like Geena," he said, then told me he knew pet owners who marked their dogs' fur with sharpies above each little sebaceous something-or-other they'd found just before taking them in to be groomed. He told Geena everything was alright, then gave me a full rundown on what to do: "Just wipe it off with hydrogen peroxide – see, it doesn't hurt her." The good doctor was cleaning the wound with hydrogen peroxide, and Geena actually seemed to be enjoying his attentions – "then put a little Neosporin on it. Just do this twice a day for the next week or so, Marc, and it will heal up in no time."

"Great," I said. "Thanks a lot, Doctor Harvey."

"Anything else I can do for you – any other concerns?" He asked.

"No, that's it" I shook my head. "I'm really glad to hear it's harmless and simple to clear up." *That was less than a ten-minute appointment!* I was thinking to myself. I was putting Geena's collar back on. *And she's fine!* I attached her leash.

Dr. Harvey grabbed the head of a doggie-shaped cookie jar sitting on a high counter. "Okay if I give her a treat?" he asked. At the word "treat," Geena's ears perked straight up and her tail started wagging. She may be ten years old, but she's still bright, especially on the subject of treats – and she still looks gorgeous, like a fluffy golden version of the old German Shepherd movie star Rin-Tin-Tin, when her ears perk straight up.

"Sure," I said. Dr. Harvey flipped the head of the doggie jar open, brought out a small milk-bone and handed it to her. She gratefully gobbled it up. "Hey, thanks again, Doctor Harvey," I said, shaking his hand.

"Sure. Anytime."

Geena and I headed for the door.

"Oh, Marc," Dr. Harvey called from behind us. Geena and I both turned back.

"Yeah?" I asked.

"Don't bother stopping at the front desk to pay," he said, waving his hand dismissively. "Just go on home and enjoy the weekend."

I was a little stunned. I just stood there. Silent. *I've been here five years already and this stuff still shocks me every time it happens*, I thought to myself, once my brain started working again. *Where I come from, that would have been twenty-five bucks minimum, probably fifty.* I didn't know what to say. I didn't want to say that. So, as in many of these Fargo moments, I found myself at a loss for words.

"Uh... Jeez..."

Dr. Harvey smiled and nodded. "Enjoy your weekend," he repeated with a big smile.

"Well, **thanks**," I said, "I certainly *will*." I realized how inadequate that sounded. Then I remembered: *Wait a minute. I figured this out a long time ago. I know exactly what to say.*

"How Fargo of you, Doctor Harvey."

"What?" He asked, tilting his head inquisitively. It reminded me of the way some dogs tilt their heads, trying to hear something a little better.

"How **Fargo** of you," I repeated.

A moment passed before a light of recognition came to his eyes. Then his head tilted back and he let out a big laugh. Still smiling, he said: "Yeah, I guess it is kinda, isn't it?"

"It sure is," I said, nodding. "*Very* Fargo of you."

*   *   *

We got our first little taste of Fargo nearly ten years ago. That remarkable story is in Chapter One. That taste stayed with us, and sure enough, we soon found ourselves moving here. That amazing story is in Chapter Two.

And the *How Fargo of You* stories just go on from there.

Now by **Fargo**, I'm not talking about anything remotely related to city limits, or even the greater metro area of about 200,000 people.   These not-so-random acts of kindness, generosity and courage are a staple of life for hundreds of miles in every direction. In these pages, you'll find a *How Fargo of You* story from Hunter, a small North Dakota town a good thirty miles northwest of Fargo, and another from the lakes country of Minnesota, about fifty miles to the east. And I've heard lots of what I insist on calling *How Fargo of You* stories from as far away as Wisconsin, Nebraska and the prairie parts of Canada directly north of us. But near as I can tell, Fargo is pretty close to the center of the remarkable Northern Prairie Culture these incidents flow from like cool, clear water gurgling out of a pristine spring.

And besides, *How Fargo of You* has a better ring to it than *How Northern Prairie of You.*

When I started telling people these *How Fargo of You* stories, it didn't matter whether they'd lived here all their lives or never been here before. For the locals, my newcomer's view seemed to help them appreciate what they had. For those who'd never experienced this part of the country, hearing what people are like around here was a *revelation.* And that's what the Northern Prairie has been for me. An ongoing revelation.

Before we came here, I didn't know there was a place where people wouldn't wonder who you were or what you thought before they'd help you, a place where people tend to think of the

15

other person without thinking too much. Before we came here, I honestly didn't know this kind of a culture – a culture of *anonymous kindness* – lay within the realm of human possibility.

This knowledge has changed me. Perhaps it will change you. And to everyone within at least a few hundred miles of this wonderful place my family and I now call home, there's only one thing I can say to fully express our thanks, only one compliment I know of that's big enough:

How Fargo of You.

CHAPTER 1

Our First Visit

You could have knocked me over with a feather.

When you leave Phoenix in June and three hours later find yourself coming into the Minneapolis-St. Paul International Airport, it's a bit of a jolt to the system. In Phoenix, a few buildings are green, and where there's a lot of watering you'll see foliage, but otherwise the general landscape ranges from a light dirt brown to a dirty light brown. Now, peering through the window of our plane onto the Twin Cities below, I felt like we were entering *Opposite World*. Laid out below me was a blanket of deep, rich green. Sure, there were beige and brown buildings dotting the landscape here and there, and an occasional patch of dirt around a construction site – though it was a lot darker, richer-looking dirt than I was used to – but everything else was *green*. I mean *really* green.

Twenty minutes later, as we walked outside into the fresh summer air, my skin tingled in the breeze. I remembered: That's what *cool* feels like. That's *moisture*.

This really is Opposite World, I thought.

I had barely begun to discover how opposite it was.

By late afternoon, we were driving a white, midsized rental car up Interstate 94 toward Fargo. Our children, Anastasia, six, and Austen, four, were in the back, oohing and aahhing at the rolling, lush, lake-dotted Minnesota countryside. They'd never seen country quite like this before. To the kids and me, it felt a little like a fairytale. To my wife Charlene, who had grown up in Northern Illinois and Wisconsin, it felt a lot like home.

It was June of 2001. We were on our way to visit my wife's best friend, Melody.

*   *   *

Not long after Melody graduated from nursing school in Arizona in 1997, she'd stayed in our home for a few months.

Her new medical job, as a surgical nurse in an eye clinic, kept her busy ten hours a day, Monday through Thursday. So we hadn't seen much of her the first few days after she moved into the spare bedroom at the back of the house.

But when Charlene, the kids and I arrived home that Friday, a delicious aroma greeted us as we opened the door. To our complete surprise, a wonderful, hot dinner was waiting for us, beautifully laid out on the dining room table. A few minutes later, as our appetites became wonderfully sated, Charlene began to notice something else: The house was cleaner than we'd ever managed to get it ourselves. And after dinner, we found the week's laundry neatly hung in the right closets and stacked on the appropriate beds.

Wow! I thought. What a way to create a great first impression as a roommate!

But I was wrong. It was no mere impression. The next Friday, it happened again. Except this time, Charlene and I were told we would be going on a date the following night, Saturday, while Melody stayed home with the kids, who had already come to adore her.

Melody was the roommate from Heaven.

Except she wasn't. She was from North Dakota. Her family had homesteaded near the southwestern corner of the state in the 1870s, a beautiful piece of rolling countryside, the picturesque Cannonball River winding through it. Melody's mother and father still spent most of the year there, managing a little over a thousand pastoral acres my family would one day come to know and love. But the rest of Melody's family had moved across the state to Fargo, where they were all practicing medical professionals, just as Melody had now become.

And so, as all things do, Melody's stay with us eventually came to an end. On a hot, dusty day in June of 1999, we sadly helped load her blue-and-white Chevy pickup for the drive back to Fargo. She had accepted a job working as a nurse in a plastic surgery institute owned by her sister and brother-in-law there. Melody was going home.

*   *   *

Now, two years later, it was our turn to stay with Melody.

About three-and-a-half hours out of Minneapolis, the lakes disappeared and the rolling hills flattened out into the Great Plains. We were nearing the Dakotas. The fairytale seemed to be disappearing. The landscape quickly became flat, dull and boring. As we came into Moorhead, Fargo's sister city on the Minnesota side of the Red River, there was little to see. Nevertheless, the mood in the car began to lighten. We were almost there! We were about to see "Aunt" Melody, as the kids called her, for the first time in two years!

We had a wonderful time catching up with Mel that evening. I'd like to say we were the kind of houseguests she'd been. That's what I'd like to say. Two little kids having just flown across the country, ridden across Minnesota, frazzled parents in tow – I'm sure we were real dream guests. At least we went to bed early. First thing in the morning, we were going to head across the state. Melody was taking us to meet her parents and spend a few days exploring the family homestead.

While the kids and Charlene were getting ready to leave the next morning, I drove the rental car down to the nearest gas station to fill up for the trip. As I approached the Petro station at 45th Street and the freeway, it looked like a thousand other gas stations I'd seen in my life. Little did I know that it was unlike any gas station I'd ever visited before. As I pulled in, there was not the slightest hint I was beginning a journey into a real fairytale world that, until then, I had never imagined possible.

I pulled up to the pump. I got out and walked around the car. I pulled my credit card out of my wallet. I went to slide it into the card reader, but couldn't find one. Then I saw the big black-and-white sign right above the pump: PLEASE PAY INSIDE. So Fargo was a few years behind Phoenix. That's to be expected, I thought. I trudged toward the front door of the Petro.

I walked inside. The place was busy and I had to get in line. When I arrived at the counter I handed my credit card to the cute girl behind the large pump-controlling console. "I need to fill up on number ten," I said.

She looked at her console and furrowed her brow. "Uh…" she said, tilting her head a little, clearly perplexed. Then she looked right at me. "But you haven't pumped yet."

You could have knocked me over with a feather.

I remember the moment as if it were this morning. It took a while for the words to sink in. Their meaning was deep. And foreign. *Very* foreign. They meant *she assumed I was a decent person.* And on an even deeper level, her words meant the company she worked for *actually trusted me.* They didn't operate on the assumption I was a criminal. For the first time in my adult life I suddenly found myself in a business transaction where I was anonymously assumed to be worthy of a little trust. It was very unfamiliar territory.

Could it really be?

"Oh..." I sputtered. "Uh, you mean... you mean you want me to fill up first, and... and *then* pay you?" I managed to blurt out.

"Yeah," she said cheerily, a small smile coming to her lips as she handed my credit card back to me, unused. This had obviously happened before. The Petro was right off the Interstate and undoubtedly served customers from other parts of the country on occasion – and she clearly *enjoyed* this part of her job. "Just fill up and then come back in and we'll take care of you." She almost sang the line, as if she were in a Rogers and Hammerstein musical.

I was speechless. I knew there was something I could say, something I *should* say. But I had no idea, yet, what it was. *How nice of you* came to mind, but fell far short of the mark. "Okay," was all I managed. I pushed out through the front door and walked back to the rental car in a daze. I was lucky no one was driving through the lot at the time, because I probably would have walked right in front of them.

But you haven't pumped yet. The words kept ringing in my head as I began to fill up.

As the pump clicked along, a smile began slowly creeping across my face. I could feel it welling up from a place deep within me, a place I hadn't felt in a long, long time. *So this is what community feels like,* I realized.

But you haven't pumped yet. I'd never heard words that sounded more beautiful.

And I've never paid for anything more happily than when I handed that girl my credit card again a few minutes later. What I got that day from her, her company and the community my family was soon to become a part of was priceless. And as long as I live, that Petro station will hold a special place in my heart.

It is, of course, completely absurd to get weepy writing a story about a gas station. So of course I'm not. But don't ever ask me to read this story out loud.

I was beginning to learn that many things I didn't know could exist actually existed. Invaluable, priceless things like trust and community and a place where the Golden Rule actually ruled, and people actually practiced it, rather than just giving it lip service – not because they had to, but because they *wanted* to.

A place where a lot of people had smiles coming from the same place mine first welled up from at the Petro pump that day.

And although I had been speechless that first morning in Fargo, soon I wasn't. Episodes like this lay around every corner for hundreds of miles in every direction, and one day, just the right phrase fell from my lips. As I heard myself say it, I knew I'd finally found the perfect way to express exactly how I felt when a person – or an organization – treated me, my wife, my kids or soon, my many Fargo friends, in exactly the way any of us would most like to be treated, if we lived in a perfect, fairytale world...

How Fargo of You.

CHAPTER 2

Moving In

You mean even teenagers here are... Fargo?

I don't remember the exact moment the words *How Fargo of You* first fell from my lips. But watching the Shanley Boys, it occurred to me there was something very *Fargo* going on. That was the first time I realized Fargo wasn't just a place, it was a quality – and that *Fargo* was just the right adjective to describe it. It all happened quite suddenly, the day we moved into our new house in Reiles Acres, a small enclave about a mile north of the city.

It was the summer of 2005 – four years since our first visit. Our kids were now eight and ten years old, and for the last couple of years in Arizona, Charlene and I had grown increasingly worried.

*   *   *

We knew that as Anastasia and Austen grew older, they'd want more freedom. They'd want to walk or ride their bikes to school or to see friends – out on the streets by themselves! They'd be attending high schools where the prevailing style was butt cracks and cleavage. Severe drug problems pervaded every high school we knew of – and little more than half the kids graduated.

I'm exaggerating slightly. *Very* slightly. My wife and I had both worked in education during the previous decade, and knew the high school dropout rate in Arizona hovered at about 40 percent – not as bad as some major U.S. cities, but that was little consolation.[1] Our children's teenage years were looming, and for us, living in the Phoenix area, they were bringing deep parental dread.

We lived in a moderately affluent neighborhood on the northwest side of the Valley of the Sun, a few miles from where I'd been raised more than 30 years earlier. The Valley had been a

---

[1] See *Notes on the Chapters* at the end of the book for more details about high school graduation rates in Arizona, North Dakota and other states.

pretty good place to be a kid then. I'd grown up in large neighborhoods that were relatively crime-free. Those kinds of neighborhoods had since disappeared. When our son attended first grade less than a block from our house, we'd felt compelled to drive him to school every day – it was just too risky to let him walk the 100 yards or so down the sidewalk by himself. A small child on the sidewalk alone was just so... *vulnerable.*

It was getting worse. A couple of reporter friends had told me there were days when as many as five or six murders were committed in the Valley, and one or two of the more "normal" homicides wouldn't make it into the newspapers or onto the television or radio news *at all. Not even a snippet.* They just weren't newsworthy. Then, in the fall of 2004, there was a cop killing on the street a couple miles from our house. Even amidst all these other worries, that stood out. We took notice.

Every day, as our kids grew, the old African proverb – *it takes a village to raise a child* – was becoming truer for us. Until now, we'd been able to keep our kids wrapped in a snug little sanctuary of home, family, friends, well-chosen caregivers and educators. But soon, our kids would start struggling to break free of those wrappings – as they should. Soon, they'd be learning about life *out there.* And Phoenix was no longer a good *out there* in which to learn anything, much less how to become a young adult. We needed to find a good *out there.*

Don't get me wrong. We had a great life. Our kids had grown up safe, secure and happy. Charlene and I both had great work lives and lots of local family and friends. By the time they were in second and fourth grade, both our kids were doing extremely well, attending a charter school run by a brilliant educator, Robert Dodd, with whose family we had become close. We had a lot of reasons to stay in the Valley.

Then, suddenly, as we entered 2005, everything started to change. A conflict in philosophy between the school's accountant and our friend, Principal Dodd, resulted in his leaving. The school's performance, by our eyes, began to decline. Also in January, my mother, who lived alone in a condo a few miles from our house, lost the sight in her right eye and needed more help. The management at my wife's place of business had changed, and eventually, she decided she wanted a change, too, submitting her resignation in February. At the same time, a major writing project I'd been working on for the previous year and a half had come to a successful conclusion, and I had nothing on the immediate horizon.

So one day in March of 2005, Charlene looked at me and said, "You know, Marc, all those things that were holding us here – the kids' school, my job, your writing project – they're not there anymore. They've just sort of disappeared. Maybe we should take a little *vacation*" – the tone in her voice rose just a bit on the word *vacation*, her eyebrows along with it – "you know, a little *vacation* up to *Fargo* in June, after the kids get out of school, and *bring your mother along.*"

Just about everything you need to know about my wife is in that last paragraph. She's a genius in all matters pragmatic, quite the opposite of her spouse. She had figured it all out, knew

28

exactly what we should do, knew exactly how we could get it done, and managed to communicate the entire message to me – not always the swiftest receiver of messages – in a few well-chosen words.

*   *   *

So on June first, 2005, almost four years to the day since our first visit, the five of us flew up to Fargo *on vacation*. We all stayed in "Aunt" Melody's lovely new house, in the small Fargo suburb of Prairie Rose. The weather was gorgeous, the landscape was green, the people were, of course, all very *Fargo*, and my mother, as Charlene knew she would, fell in love. By the end of our first week *on vacation*, we were looking at houses large enough for all five of us to move into together before school started back up – less than three short months away.

When our return tickets came due on June 15, we hadn't found a place, so Charlene stayed on with Melody to keep looking. The kids, my mother and I all flew back down to Phoenix, where over the next six weeks we sold our two places, packed up and got out of Dodge before the gunfights got any worse. While we were doing that, Charlene found us a great house in a wonderful little family community about a mile north of Fargo called Reiles Acres, and got a job working at Microsoft's second largest field campus in the world, located in South Fargo.

So, on an early August morning, we watched an immense moving van stuffed with everything from our old house and my mother's condo approaching our new home. We were all brimming with excitement – the kids, Charlene, my mom and me. It had been a whirlwind summer.

"Melody's coming over with some Shanley boys," Charlene chirped as I watched the huge moving van barely make the corner onto our street, tires over the curbs.

"Some what?" I asked.

"Shanley boys."

"Brothers named *Chandler* or something?" I asked stupidly, preoccupied with the belongings of our lives teetering near sloping 5-foot-deep drainage ditches contoured into the lawns along both sides of our street.

"No, I think Shanley's the name of a school. It was Melody's idea. She says they're coming to help."

That was good enough. If the Shanley Boys were Mel's idea, they were welcome. And looking at the 12-foot-high, 40-foot-long truck now safely back on the asphalt – a truck I had personally helped stuff, top-to-bottom, back in Phoenix – I knew we needed all the help we could get.

Five minutes later, our world was rapidly transforming. Four big, friendly, muscular young men were parading our worldly possessions through our garage, into our new home. I stood there, a bit dumbfounded, off to one side of the garage, between Charlene and Mel.

"I love young men," Melody laughed, admiring a couple of fantastically great-looking guys as a couch they were carrying went by.

The couch was followed by a love seat held aloft by just one young guy, directly under its center, holding it up the way a power-lifter holds a barbell, way over his head. As he went through the garage with a big smile, he asked, "Where do you want this, Charlene?"

"That goes in the living room, Gary," my wife said, in a very familiar tone.

"Okay!" said Gary, bounding effortlessly up the small flight of stairs leading into the house, lowering the loveseat and tilting it slightly to get it through the door at just the right moment, balanced perfectly the whole time.

"Who's Gary?" I asked, more bewildered by the minute. "I didn't know you *knew* any of these Chandley Boys, honey." The name Chandley, or Shanley, or whatever it was, was quickly taking on almost mystical connotations.

Charlene and Melody both laughed. "Gary's not a Shanley Boy," Melody said. "He's a friend."

"How much are we supposed to pay them?" I asked Mel.

"I didn't say anything about money," Mel said. "I just told them I had some friends who'd just moved to Fargo and could probably use some help moving in. They said they had a softball game in the afternoon, but they were free in the morning, so they'd be over."

I didn't know whether to laugh or cry, so I just stood there, more dumbfounded. Fargo has that effect on me a lot, to this day.

Over the next half hour, as the moving van continued to empty and our house fill up almost as if by magic, I got filled in as well. Gary was a friend of Melody's, in his early twenties. The other three strapping young men – Adam, Brian and Nick – were recent graduates of Shanley, the local Catholic high school.

But don't get the wrong idea. Melody's dad is a retired Methodist Minister. Charlene, my wife, is Lutheran. Gary, I think, believes in break dancing. My religious views float somewhere between George Washington's and Einstein's, depending on how many fortuitous coincidences – like all the things that had been holding us in Phoenix disappearing almost overnight – I've experienced lately. And back in Phoenix, I'd known a number of students and graduates of the largest Catholic high school, Brophy Prep. While I thought highly of many of them, I honestly couldn't imagine any of them doing something like this at the drop of a hat for someone they'd never met. Things like that just never happened in Phoenix, or California, or anywhere else I'd ever lived.

This was *Fargo.*

Man, did we find a good out there, or what?, I was thinking to myself as I ran around trying to help these great guys do all our work for us. We'd known that North Dakota had about the lowest high school drop out rate in the nation. That was one of the many reasons Charlene had suggested we come here *on vacation.* But the qualities Gary and the Shanley boys were demonstrating can't be described in statistical terms – not even close.

About an hour in, the truck was already halfway unloaded – a job the driver, with years of experience, had said would take a good four hours. Suddenly, Charlene caught me by the shirtsleeve. "I'm going into town to buy some stuff to make sandwiches," she said. "I'll be back in about a half hour."

By noon, the truck was fully unloaded and Charlene had laid a huge spread out on the newly installed dining room table, a beautiful array of lunch meats, breads, condiments and chips.

"Wow! How awesome!" Brian said, his eyes wide as saucers. "You didn't have to do this..." The other guys chimed in with similar reactions – *they were honestly surprised!* It was another laugh or cry moment. They'd been working tirelessly all morning for us – people they had never heard of before their casual acquaintance, Melody, had mentioned something a day or two earlier – and now, they were genuinely appreciative that we were going so far as to – *gee!* – feed them.

After a great lunch, during which we learned as much about these guys as we could – which wasn't a whole lot because they didn't like talking with their mouths full – we almost needed a crowbar to get a $20 bill into each of their hands. If they hadn't worn themselves out with all their hard work, we might not have succeeded.

Our kids, of course, had taken it all in. *Drink it in,* I thought, *drink it in.* And I've been thinking that ever since. Instead of dreading having our kids out and about, as we did back in Phoenix, we now relish it. Get *out there – out there is* **good.**

So, hey, Adam, Brian, Gary and Nick – we want you to know you did a lot more for us than help move our worldly possessions. You helped us with possessions infinitely more valuable. It was all so fast, and so astounding, that we really didn't know how to thank you properly at the time. But now, we know exactly what to say:

How Fargo of You.

CHAPTER 3

The Carpenter of Divinity

Bringing wonder in through a doggie door.

We needed a doggie door. Yesterday.

Sport and Geena are Golden Retriever mixes who came up from Arizona with us, tipping the scales at a little over eighty pounds each. They're used to having their own door, and the human members of our family like that arrangement as well. We subscribe to the school of canine etiquette that goes something like, "Doormen are for VIPs at fancy hotel entrances; dogs find their own way in and out of the backyard."

So I went looking for a doggie door that could handle a twenty-below arctic blast. Not surprisingly, I couldn't find any manufacturers that made such a promise. But once I found the best I could, I called Melody.

"Hey Mel, what's the name of that carpenter friend of yours we ran into at the *32 Below* concert in June?" (*32 Below* is the name of a band from Fargo; it doesn't get that cold here in June.)

"Oh, *John*. Do you need something?"

"Yeah, I need a doggie door put in. I already bought it. I just need it put in by someone who knows what they're doing."

"Hold on, I've got his number right here…"

John came by mid-afternoon the next day. As soon as I opened the door, I recognized his big, friendly smile. He seemed surprisingly fresh for having already put in a full eight hours on a house he was building, but I figured he was just coming by to reconnoiter and give me an estimate. I showed him the big box containing the **Heavy Duty Deluxe Large Dog Door** I'd bought. Then I showed him where Charlene and I had decided we'd like it to go, an area to the side of and under the kitchen bar, leading out onto the backyard deck.

To my surprise, there was no estimate or talk of money. Instead, John started sawing a hole in the wall. We really needed a doggie door, so I didn't stop him.

"You want me to open the box and get the stuff out for you?" I offered. "I'll make sure I don't tear it," I added, since he was going off the schematic printed on the back.

"That'd be great!" he said, with the big friendly smile.

John was the epitome of efficiency, and within ten minutes or so I was looking at our deck through a large rectangle cut through both the wall and the exterior metal siding.

"Man, that's a thick wall," John said, grabbing the tape measure off his belt. "It's framed with two-by-sixes!" The tape zipped back into its case as he stood up and headed out to his truck. I decided to follow, leaving the contents of the doggie door laid out on the floor.

As I walked out the front door I saw his truck for the first time, beautifully scripted lettering *Skarphol and Sons* along the side. I didn't know John's last name, or anything else about him. After a moment's reflection I decided it might embarrass him to assume he owned his own company, if that wasn't the case. I opted for the alternative approach: "Is that who you work for during normal hours?"

"Odd hours, too," John answered, big smile flashing. "That's me. No sons with me right at the moment. Didn't think a doggie door would call for it!" He laughed a big, hearty laugh while grabbing a two-by-six out of the back of his truck, turning and heading back in. I continued following.

As we got back to the jobsite, John glanced at the contents I'd laid out on the floor and immediately announced: "We have a problem."

"What's that?" I asked.

"The bolts that come with the doggie door aren't long enough for your thick walls."

"Alright, I'll run into town and get some."

"You probably won't find any long enough. I'll have to make them."

"*Make* them?" I asked, wondering if I'd heard right.

"Yeah, here's what we need," he said, jotting down the diameter of the bolts the doggie door required. "If they don't have any bolts this diameter that are at least..." – he glanced at the schematic on the back of the doggie door box – "...at least eleven inches long, you'll have to buy two threaded dowels this diameter and a dozen nuts to fit them. While you're getting that stuff I'll frame up the wall."

Off I went. John was right, none of the three main hardware outlets in town (all fairly close to each other, thank goodness) had bolts of the necessary diameter longer than eight inches. I ended up at Mac's, the locally owned hardware store, buying two 3-foot-long threaded dowels and a dozen nuts to go with them. I arrived back home about an hour after leaving. The rectangle in the wall was now beautifully finished, two-by-sixes perfectly framing the inside of the wall. John was just hanging out with the dogs, waiting for me to get back.

I handed him the dowels, and he set to work with a hacksaw, cutting bolts to fit. I suddenly remembered something Melody had told me.

"Melody said you lived in Tempe for a while." Tempe is a suburb of Phoenix, across town from Glendale, where we had been living before our recent *vacation*.

"Yeah, we lived there for a while back in the eighties."

"What were you doing in Tempe?" I asked.

"Going to school," John said as the first measured bolt clanged onto his little workbench.

"Oh. What did you study?" I persisted.

"I got my bachelor's in non-profit work there, which was my first degree," John said, sawing through another bolt.

"You have others?"

"Yeah. Eventually I went into a doctoral program and got a degree in ministry."

"Are you serious?" I asked, stupidly. I could tell he wasn't joking.

"Yeah," John replied with a chuckle, smile flashing.

I still wasn't sure I'd heard right. "So... did you get a *doctorate*?"

"Yeah." *Clang.* Down went another bolt.

"A doctorate in...?"

"Ministry." He replied, as simply as possible for me, lining up the next bolt.

"So that's like religious studies, right? Kind of like a doctor of divinity kind of a thing?"

"Yeah," he said with another chuckle, "kind of like that." The last bolt fell from his hacksaw, clanging onto the workbench. It was the perfect punctuation.

There wasn't much left for me to do but watch John's deft hands assemble the pieces of the doggie door as I contemplated the implications of having a carpenter with a doctorate in ministry. *Maybe if you really understand Jesus,* I speculated to myself, *you become a carpenter.* But as John tightened the last bolt on our beautiful, custom-installed doggie door, my mind came back down to more earthly wonderings.

"What do I owe you?" I asked as he started putting his tools away. I braced myself, because with all the extra work caused by the need for custom-fitted bolts, it had been a little over three hours since he'd arrived – and I knew by the clear mastery of his craft that he couldn't be cheap.

"It's a housewarming gift." He said, flashing the big smile.

"Huh?" was all I heard myself say. Looking back on it, I'm sure John enunciated the words clearly. But no meaning arrived. My brain wasn't accepting.

"You don't owe me anything," he said, shaking his head. *"It's a housewarming gift."* The meaning began to seep in.

"Uhh… no, John, you've been here three hours and there was a lot of extra work, with the custom-fitted bolts and all…"

He stood up and flashed the big grin once more, putting his hand out to shake mine. "Welcome to *Fargo.*"

*   *   *

It might have been later that evening, gazing at that doggie door, still in a slightly euphoric daze, thinking about what it meant to be a carpenter in the 21st Century with a Ph.D. in religious studies who was clearly expert at practicing both, wondering over our great good fortune at finding ourselves in this wonderful place, that the phrase first began wedging itself, like a shim for balance, into my brain…

How Fargo of You.

CHAPTER 4

The First Law of Winter

The colder it is, the warmer it gets.

For me, snow existed in places people went to go skiing.

I'd never been through four seasons in my life. In Arizona, California and Florida, where I'd lived until now, sure, it was hot in the summer. And it was cool in the winter, *sometimes* – the same way it's cool, sometimes, during the *summer* in Fargo. If you shut your eyes and tried real hard, in the places I'd spent my first fifty years, you could imagine there were two seasons –

Hot and *Cooler*. That worked pretty well until you opened your eyes, looked outside, and tried to figure out what time of year it was. Everything looked pretty much the same year-round. And we all lived inside air-conditioned spaces, from houses to offices to vehicles, a good nine months out of the year. So for me, the seasons had always been more an act of the imagination than of nature.

Snow had always been something to be visited. But now, it was about to be visited upon us.

In early October, people started asking, "Are you ready for winter yet?" At first, I thought this was a figurative sort of question, a sort of friendly Fargo shorthand for *Have you mentally braced yourself, warm-blooded novice?* But I soon realized it was much more. It was a deep and abiding concern for my family's survival.

This began to hit home sometime in early October, when a new acquaintance asked, "Do you have a snow blower?"

"A what?" I responded, brilliantly.

It quickly became clear that October was a time of fairly intense preparation for everyone around here, and I was woefully unprepared. Winter was coming, ready *or not*. There were an uncertain number of days before it hit, and a certain number of things had to be done before it did, or it would be *too late*. We could be in real trouble.

So October became busy. Buying winter clothes – hats, jackets, snow pants, socks and boots – for everyone, all good to at least twenty below. Bringing *everything* inside – barbeques, patio furniture, hoses, dog toys, *everything* – and getting it organized well enough to still walk through the garage, leaving room for our two vehicles. Getting a garage heater installed, so nothing out there would get completely frozen. Covering all the outside faucets so our plumbing wouldn't die a frozen death. Buying a snow blower, getting it put together and practice-running it, so my first time behind the handles wouldn't be in ten-below weather with the snow falling sideways in a twenty-mile-an-hour wind. Buying a generator and getting it primed and running, ready to go at a moment's notice in case of an extended power outage. Getting a custom dog house (care of the Carpenter of Divinity) put in around the outside of the doggie door so it wouldn't get covered over in the snow drifts to come. I even consulted the top Fargo engineer for Xcel, the gas company, and confirmed that if the power went out for a few days, as I'd learned it could when an ice storm topples major power lines, the natural gas would still flow. Then we went into town and picked out a nice gas fireplace, which was installed just in time, as it turned out.

Whew – we were ready. I hoped. October ended with our kids enjoying their first Fargo Halloween trick-or-treating with an occasional snowflake or two on their noses.

The first real test came in late November, a few days after our new fireplace had finally been installed. About mid-afternoon on Sunday the 28th, it started to rain, a cold rain that soon became a *freezing* rain – warmer upper clouds were releasing droplets, but a colder, lower layer had brought the

THE FIRST LAW OF WINTER

temperature of everything on the ground – trees, streets, houses, everything – to below freezing. As soon as the rain hit, it turned to ice. And as we went to bed that night, it was still raining.

When we got up Monday morning, the rain had turned to sleet, which was blowing sideways in winds between twenty and thirty miles per hour – exact measurements were impossible, the television meteorologist reported, because all the anemometers were frozen over in ice. And all the schools were closed.

"Our first snow day!!! Yeah!!!" the kids chorused, then Austen added: "And it's not even snowing!!!"

That was about to change.

Midafternoon, the sleet turned to snow. The winds had picked up to about forty miles per hour, the meteorologist now guesstimated, with gusts even higher. We were in the midst of our first Fargo blizzard. For a while, we all stood at the big living room picture window. Nothing but white. Occasionally, a ghostlike image of the big trees across the street would appear briefly, then disappear in another gust of blowing snow. It was eerie, magical, and absolutely fascinating for the kids and me, whose eyes had never seen such things. Charlene, of course, couldn't have been happier. By evening, she was fully settled in, warm and cozy by the fire, reading a book, cookies baking in the oven. She was home, and so were we all.

Little did I realize it was just the beginning. Only as the long, cold winter wore on would we discover how truly magical, warm and cozy a Fargo winter can be. The first revelation was right around the corner.

We slept in Tuesday morning. No one would be going anywhere for a while, local newscasters had assured us the night before. The snow and wind would settle down, but Fargo would be covered not just in a thick blanket of snow, but even more troublesome, beneath the snow would be layer upon layer of slick ice, first laid down by the freezing rain, then added to by the sleet that had followed. Even snowplows would have trouble navigating what promised to be *extremely* slippery streets. Fargo would be digging out for a while.

So it was about nine in the morning before I walked to the living room picture window and began pulling the cord to open the blinds. About halfway, I dropped the cord and simply stood in awe. The world outside, which had been green and gold just two days ago, then completely white yesterday, had once again transformed, this time into something completely unexpected – a silvery blue landscape with hundreds of sparks of golden sunlight glinting off of everything, sparks that shot and danced and glistened with even the slightest movement. The world was made of glass!

Breaking out of my reverie, I ran down and woke the kids. Soon we were out exploring this strange, new fairytale world. The sky was a cloudless azure, the sun a deep yellow. Even the stop sign at the corner of our street was beautiful, washed completely clean and covered in an inch-thick glaze of ice that made it look like a giant, delicious cherry-red lollipop sticking out of a whipped-cream world. Looking around, our whole neighborhood was strewn with glistening colored candy houses with generous helpings of white icing poured over them. Austen suddenly yelled, "We're walking on a giant *cake!*" and we all laughed. Best of all were the trees, covered in nearly an inch of clear-blue ice, shooting golden sparks of sunlight whenever they swayed ever so slightly, crackling – you could actually hear them – in the tiniest of breezes.

Wow. So the worst Fargo storms were actually – *the best!*

This was the first paradox of Fargo winter I discovered. But it was not the last. Nor the greatest. For I was soon to learn the law of winter in Fargo.

*   *   *

It was a February afternoon, a little over two months since our first magical winter storm. A light snow had been falling since morning.

I was a bit late getting home. *Charlene's probably been home about a half-hour already*, I thought, turning into our driveway.

As I walked into the kitchen, Charlene greeted me. "Hi, Honey! I got stuck in our driveway! I told you to snow blow the driveway before going out so it wouldn't build up *all day!*"

She had that half-quizzical, *Why didn't you listen?*, half-comical, *Because you were on Planet Marc!* look I know so well.

"If you got stuck, why aren't you still out there?" I asked.

Charlene whacked me on the shoulder, trying not to laugh. "Because a *neighbor* rescued me! He pushed the car back out onto the street, then drove his big snow blower over and cleared the driveway. Didn't you notice there isn't any snow on the driveway?

"Umm... Now that you mention it, I guess there should be snow on the driveway."

"You *think?*"

"On occasion," I said, "although this apparently isn't one of them." The kids started laughing. They'd moved into the kitchen as soon as they'd heard me come home. They loved the *dad's in trouble* routine, and I was grateful; Charlene can't resist breaking a smile when both our kids are laughing. She turned toward the counter to hide her face. I was supposed to be in *trouble*, not making everyone laugh.

My mind, however, was still on the story of Charlene's adventure. "So who rescued you?" I asked.

"I don't know his name." She turned around and pointed east, a little smile still showing. "He came from two houses down. He was out snowblowing his driveway when I got stuck. Next thing I knew he was over, smiling and pushing the car back out onto the street and telling me to wait. Then he ran back to his place and brought his big snow blower over and cleared out our entire driveway." She was looking at me, eyes wide, giving me her 'Can you believe *that?*' look. "I mean, what a *super* nice guy!"

That weekend, I made a point of introducing myself to our gallant neighbor two houses to the east, a North Dakota native named Chad. As I came to know him a little better over the next few years, I learned that Chad is one of those Northern Prairie, farm-raised guys who's remarkably capable and generous, but who never seems to notice how good – in every sense of the word – he is. When I brought him a thank you card our whole family had signed, he was all smiles, playing down his act of kindness, shaking his head, waving his hand dismissively, "Oh, it was nothing. *Really.*"

And that's how Chad introduced us to the governing law of Fargo in winter:

The colder it is, the warmer it gets.

Post Script: As soon as I started writing this story, nearly four years to the day since Chad rescued Charlene from our snowy driveway, it occurred to me we hadn't really given Chad a very *Fargo* thank you at the time. I guess I hadn't quite caught on yet. So as I finished writing this chapter last night, we all baked cookies, and earlier today, we put the cookies in a gift bag along with a copy of this story and took them over to Chad's, with a little card that read, of course…

How Fargo of You.

CHAPTER 5

Road Construction Season

These people are serious.

There's an old saying in this part of the country that goes something like this: If you're familiar with all four seasons: almost winter, winter, still winter *and Road Construction...* you might live in North Dakota! That's what this story's about, sort of. For it wasn't until our first full summer... umm, I mean, during our first full season of *Road Construction,* that I began to *fully* realize just how differently people around here behaved from any community of human beings I'd ever experienced.

One of the first things I noticed about Fargo was that every driver had a lot more roadway to work with than anywhere else I'd ever been. The *worst* traffic day in Fargo is *far* better than the *best* traffic day in Phoenix, L.A., Florida or a host of other places I've visited, from big cities like Atlanta and Chicago to small towns like Payson, Arizona and Ashland, Oregon. I'm not kidding. That is, as long as there aren't any blizzard conditions. Oh, and until summ... I mean, until *Road Construction Season*. Because once road construction starts, as many as a fifth of the streets are no longer available. They're under construction. I don't mean a little fix up here and there. I mean *Under Road Construction*.

It's the end of May as I write this, and two out of the five routes I can take from Reiles Acres into Fargo have become unavailable in the last three weeks – and may very well remain so until the end of summer, although that's unlikely; they work fast around here. They have to. *Almost winter* is coming.

The weather up here plays havoc with roadways. So when the five months suitable for roadwork come around – about May through September – construction crews are suddenly everywhere, and so are the detours. In mid-May of 2006, after experiencing my fifth or sixth detour of the day, none of which had been in place a couple of weeks earlier, I remember thinking, *these people are **serious**.* Noting the earnestness with which roads were repaired and improved, however, was just a prelude to a much bigger revelation.

I'd just finished some errands in the south end of Fargo. Heading for home, I got on Interstate 29, traveling north through the middle of town. But as I came up and over a crest in the freeway at the 13th Avenue exit, I suddenly saw orange cones ahead. Lots of them. As far as the eye could see. The cones were narrowing the four northbound lanes down to one lane on the left – normally the "fast' lane, which now looked to be creeping along at a few miles per hour in the distance.

I was in the middle lane, so I immediately put my blinker on and, as soon as it was safe, eased into the left lane and began slowing down to match the speed of the cars up ahead. This was the courteous thing to do.

I'd become a courteous driver about ten years earlier, when Charlene was pregnant with our first child. It was the result of a sudden influx of sanity demanded by nature, a gift of late fatherhood, I suppose. But back in Arizona, being a courteous driver had been a very lonely job description. If you were a courteous driver and wanted to remain a courteous driver, I'd quickly learned, you got used to being taken advantage of *all the time*.

So once I eased into the left lane of I-29 and started slowing down, I expected at least a couple dozen cars to whiz by on my right, speeding the half mile or so ahead to where the orange cones finally narrowed down to one lane. Then these drivers, I knew, would cut in to the single lane of traffic remaining, adding further delay to anyone silly enough, like me, to be a courteous driver.

That's what had always happened, everywhere I'd ever lived. It was the norm. It was to be expected.

But nobody went by.

This was completely foreign to my decades of road-faring experience. I checked the rear view mirror. I could see several dozen cars behind me. They were all slowing and, as I had, easing over into the left lane in order. Like me, they were all doing this a good half-mile before they were actually forced to do so by the orange cones.

I looked ahead. There were at least fifty cars and trucks directly ahead of me in the left lane, even though the orange cones were still wide enough to accommodate two lanes of traffic for another quarter-mile or so. We were down to a slow crawl of maybe five to ten miles an hour. But no one took advantage of the situation – and the courteousness of the other drivers – to cut ahead.

So I waited. Surely at least one or two cars would come whizzing by.

But I just kept waiting.

Looking at the courteous, relaxed drivers ahead and behind me, I started wondering if I was losing my grip on reality. I snuck a furtive glance over my shoulder just to make sure Rod Serling wasn't smoking a cigarette in the back seat, hosting an episode of the *Twilight Zone*.

It took another two or three minutes of slow crawl before I reached the spot where the orange cones narrowed to a single lane alongside my minivan. And yet, from the time I'd first come over the crest in the freeway and eased into the left lane, not one car had gone by me on my right.

Not one.

If this had been a dream and I'd awoken right then, I would have turned to Charlene and said, "I just had the *weirdest* dream." But it wasn't a dream. I was wide awake.

Until that moment, I had honestly never imagined that such behavior was humanly possible.

It's one thing when your neighbors treat you nicely. Or your friends. Or your colleagues. Or members of your church. They're you're *neighbors*. Your *friends*. Your *colleagues*. *Members of your church*. They know you, and you know them. It's clearly *in their own interests* to treat you well. This can have wonderful ramifications. Adam Smith covered these in a little book he called *The Wealth of Nations* back in, gee, what was it? Oh yeah, 1776. So in a friendly neighborhood like Reiles Acres, for instance, a sort of juggernaut of helpfulness builds up, where so much assistance and good will goes around that the generosity practically seems to flood the yards from time to time.

But a freeway is a completely different kind of environment. It's *anonymous*. So its basic nature is quite different from a neighborhood, a school, an office, or a church. Chances are, you don't know anyone occupying any of the hundred or so vehicles creeping along at five miles per hour in the left lane, with the right lane open for a good half-mile ahead. There aren't any obvious bad personal consequences that will come from not keeping the order in which you arrived at the delay, but instead, cutting ahead the hundred or so places – and eliminating several minutes' wait – before the orange cones force you to merge.

If you cut ahead, of course, it slows the flow of traffic for everyone else, stopping the whole line of cars momentarily while you merge. But everywhere else I'd ever lived, everyone else was not a high priority. If the orange cones were two lanes wide, it was like they were crying out, "Take advantage of the situation while you can," and lot of people listened.

But no one on this Fargo freeway was listening to the orange cones. They were listening to an unwritten set of road rules, elevated well above those in any state or federal driving statutes – and even, apparently, above the laws of economics described by Adam Smith.

These people are applying the golden rule **anonymously,** I realized. Once again, I heard myself thinking **these people are serious.** And once again, I felt a smile welling up from the same, deep place I had back at the Petro station on 45th Street, my first morning in Fargo: *So this is what community feels like.* And once again, I marveled at our great good fortune in finding ourselves here.

I didn't yet know the half of it.

A month or so later, I was driving north again, along the same stretch of I-29. I wasn't paying much attention. I'd been through the narrowing of the lanes a few times now, and it had become routine – so much so that this time, the orange cones failed to impinge sufficiently on my consciousness. I was thinking about something, and it wasn't the road. As Charlene might say, I was on *Planet Marc*.

I suddenly found myself whizzing by cars on my left, cars I'd been keeping pace with just moments before. With horror, I realized I was doing what few in Fargo were rude enough to do: I was cutting ahead to where the orange cones narrowed to a single lane. I started slowing just in time to come to a stop at the point where I could go no further: I had to interrupt the flow of traffic and cut in. Of course, *I was the only one.* I was deeply embarrassed.

With trepidation, I raised my left hand, trying to gesture "sorry" – then looked over at the line of cars to my left, fearing the scorn on the faces of other drivers I so richly deserved. But to my amazement, I saw no expression of discontent on anyone's face *whatsoever.* The only person who seemed to be paying any attention to me at all was the man in the large pickup next to my van, who had stopped and was actually *smiling* – I couldn't believe it – *smiling and waving me ahead.*

I could hardly move my foot to press down on the accelerator. It was the most stunning Fargo moment I had yet experienced. This was *the moment* when I began to truly appreciate just *how* special Fargo is.

My mind was a complete blank. About five minutes and three miles further down the road, as the freeway opened back up to three lanes, I finally began to get over the shock and awe of the amazing decency I had just been at the receiving end of – and as I returned to normal freeway speed on the last leg of my journey home, the first thought that began seeping into my mind was one of the most radical I've ever had: *The truth is*, I thought, *if Jesus or Buddha were to hang out around here for a while, they'd say we were doing* **alright**. *Not great – Jesus and Buddha, after all, had amazingly high standards for what they considered acceptable human behavior. (Love your enemies? Love your enemies!) But I honestly think, if either one of them spent a few days anonymously milling around here, they'd say we were doing* **alright**.

This was so different from any thought I could ever remember having during the fifty years and six months or so of my life leading up to that moment, it wasn't easy driving the rest of the way home. It was quite a jolt. I'm not sure I'm over it yet, nearly four years later.

Because nothing in the four years since has shaken that belief. Not a tiny tremor. In fact, it has only been reinforced, time and again. I am still amazed by this, even as I write it. Before no one sailed by me in the empty lane to my right, I had never imagined that a wide community of people would consistently behave with that sort of fairness and respect toward one another, having little more in common than a geographic area. And before that wonderful man smiled and waved me ahead, surrounded by other drivers doing a fabulous job of not noticing what a jerk I'd been, I'd never imagined that kind of instant, anonymous, friendly forgiveness to be something we could achieve as human beings. I mean, sure, I'd always had little airy-fairy daydreams that someday we might evolve in that direction. But if we ever got there we'd no longer really be human, would we? Before my first season of Fargo Road Construction, I would have considered the idea of a few hundred thousand human beings within a few hundred miles of each another treating each other this way – *with anonymous kindness* – well, I would have considered that notion a bit ridiculous. But the 1500 or so days since my two freeway epiphanies have confirmed that these were not freak incidents, but the norm in this community of people my family and I are lucky enough to have found ourselves living amongst.

*   *   *

In my mind, I see Jesus and Siddhartha driving anonymously in and around Fargo together, maybe in an old Corvair convertible with the top down (since neither would be very worried about dying – and somehow, in my head, that old Corvair has just the right look for the two of them). And every few minutes or so – like when someone heading in a different direction arrives at a stop sign before they do, but still insists on waving them ahead (an illegal kindness which is far and away the most irritating thing that happens with any regularity on the roads around here) one of them says, with a little chuckle…

*"Oh… How **Fargo** of You."*

61

CHAPTER 6

North Dakota Politics

An oxymoron?

I had no idea what was being said. But I could tell the guys who were saying it knew what they were talking about.

It was an October evening, 2006. We'd lived in Fargo just over a year now. I was feeling very settled in and happy. If you'd have asked me earlier that evening if I thought Fargo still held any major surprises for me, I would have said no. If you'd have asked me if I'd moved beyond Fargo culture shock, I would have said yes. And I would have been wrong on both counts.

It was about 9 p.m. at night, and I was running a late errand in the minivan, heading south on a nearly empty Interstate 29 toward downtown Fargo. I'd just turned on Prairie Public, North Dakota's public radio station.

I found myself listening to something like this:

First guy: "Well, Doug's got a good point there, I can see why he'd suggest we should... (some complicated tweak of agricultural policy *I couldn't remotely follow*), but I think we're a bit better off the way we're currently (another complicated description of Ag policy *I couldn't remotely follow*) because that way, (another in-depth description of likely consequences *I couldn't remotely follow*)."

Second guy: "Yeah, I see Roger's point with that, but if instead of... (description of current agricultural policy *I couldn't remotely follow*) we tried... (description of a new agricultural policy *I also couldn't remotely follow*), then... (another very logical description of likely consequences *I couldn't remotely follow*), and I think North Dakota over the long run would probably benefit more from... (the likely consequences of his suggestion *I couldn't remotely follow*) rather than... (the likely consequences of the other guy's suggestion *I couldn't remotely follow*).

I could hardly understand any of it. But I couldn't bring myself to change the station, either. It was just so different from anything I'd ever heard on the radio *in my life*. It wasn't dumbed-down for normal listeners in the least. I was clearly listening to two experts discussing the finer points of North Dakota agricultural policy, and if I couldn't follow along, that was my tough luck. In my mind, I saw thousands of farmers sitting in rapt attention in living rooms across the state, hanging on every word. But I could only follow about one word out of every five. What was I listening to?

It suddenly began to dawn on me: *Could this be some kind of a political debate?*

I listened more closely. No. It couldn't be a political debate. You couldn't tell any party differences. It wasn't ideological in the least. It was pragmatic. And way too smart. No, it wasn't politics. It was two experts who clearly respected each other's views drawing subtle distinctions between some of the options available regarding North Dakota agricultural policy.

But who were they and why were they having this discussion? My curiosity kept me listening. But after a few more minutes of only understanding about every fifth word, I gave up. I reached over to press some button, any button, to go to another station – any other station. But just before my finger pressed, I heard a third voice: "You're listening to a debate between Democrat Roger Johnson and Republican Doug Goehring," a moderator was now saying, "for the office of

65

Agricultural Commissioner, generally considered the second most important elected office in the state of North Dakota." The moderator then asked the men another question, but I didn't hear it. I was stunned. Another Fargo moment had just slapped me upside the head. I felt dazed.

And then I just started to laugh. Howl. Tears coming down my face. *Maybe I should pull off the freeway,* I thought to myself, *even though, at 9 pm on a weekday night, it's virtually **deserted.***

Looking around at the several-football-fields-worth of freeway I had to myself and thinking about what freeways looked like at 9 pm in every other place I'd ever lived, I began to laugh even harder. *I'm experiencing Fargo overload,* I realized, and my body began to convulse as I tried to stifle the bizarre, high-pitched peals my body was now emitting, like some out-of-control hyena. I barely managed to put my blinker on and get over to the right lane to take the next exit.

One of the candidates was once again saying what a smart fellow the other guy was. *I'm listening to a North Dakota **debate**,* I reminded myself. I wouldn't have thought it was possible, but I started laughing even *harder.* I started to shriek like a stuck pig.

The accumulated culture shock of the last year, our first year in Fargo, was catching up with me all at once. Hearing my first North Dakota political debate was pushing me over the edge.

North Dakota politics is oxymoronic! I couldn't help thinking, convulsing even harder, barely able to hold onto the wheel.

*Oxymoronic and... **brilliant!*** I was snorting between every gale now, uncontrollably. *Snortage... Houston, we have Snortage...*

The fear of death began to seep in, but then suddenly, I saw the headlines: *Man from Elsewhere Loses Control Listening to North Dakota Ag Debate, Dies in Flames* and I started laughing so hard I began to squeak. It was a sound I'd never heard my body make before. I could barely see the road through the tears in my eyes, but somehow managed to pull off the freeway, onto the exit ramp for Main Avenue.

Then, the last guy to receive another compliment from his opponent thanked him, and they began chuckling. *Oh no*, I thought to myself, *I can't laugh any more. I have to stop laughing.* If I'd have had any sense, I would have shut the radio off. But by this time, I was incapable of rational thought. My mind and body were a battleground, laughter and fear duking it out.

Then the guy who'd just thanked the other launched back into a complex description of agricultural policy.

*Except for all the compliments these two guys keep lavishing on each other, I can't understand a **word!*** I clung to the wheel as my body convulsed again. I could barely keep the minivan on the curve of the off ramp.

But adrenaline was kicking in now. I couldn't hear the "debate" any more – my mind was finally focusing on survival. I was able to apply my foot to the brake and come to a stop at the end of the exit ramp. Through the tears in my eyes I saw a golden, glowing empty parking lot to my right, at the Hardee's drive-thru. *Thank God*, I thought to myself. Seeing no oncoming traffic, I turned right onto Main Avenue and then right again into the Hardees. I stopped the minivan, put it into park and fell back in my seat, exhausted.

I really lost it, I thought to myself. And with that, I broke out in laughter all over again.

Eventually, I began to regain my composure. The complex, complimentary "debate" was still going on. It was more detailed than any lecture I could remember attending in college. I thought about the hundreds of millions of people living in big cities who thought of farmers as hicks. Then I thought about the level of political debate most of those folks are used to. Then I listened to these guys again.

I shook my head.

Republicans and Democrats from other areas of the country could learn a thing or two from these guys, I thought to myself, my mind beginning to come back to me. *These guys are clearly experts in the subject of the office they're running for. They're clearly concerned about really figuring out the right thing to do. They're not dumbing anything down for anyone. They don't question the other candidate's motivations. And because of all that, they don't get caught up in their own exaggerations, their own staging, to the point that they begin to think of each other as representing good and evil.*

Then suddenly I realized: *They're breaking all the most basic, unwritten rules of party politics!*

I turned the engine off and listened harder.

I could not tell which was the Republican named Doug and which the Democrat named Roger. As far as I could tell, there was no way to figure it out unless you knew their voices.

What would happen if this kind of approach spread to other parts of the country? I wondered. Then: *I'm sure high party officials on both sides wouldn't stand for such "unwarranted behavior" for a minute.*

Like I said, the Republicans and Democrats from other areas of the country could learn a thing or two from these guys.

*   *   *

Over the last five years, I've met many of the major political figures in North Dakota. I didn't set out to do this. But if you hang around this very friendly, congenial state of just over a half-million people for a while and get invited to a party here and there, you're bound to bump into your elected officials every so often, along with almost everyone else.

I'm not going to tell any tales out of school, but I will say this: The worst thing I've heard said about a Democrat since I've lived here came from an important person in the Democratic party – it was a complaint about nasty campaign tactics being used in a presidential primary in another state. And, not coincidentally, the worst thing I've heard any North Dakotan say about a Republican came from a well-placed Republican, and was equally innocuous.

So you can imagine my excitement a few months ago, in late April of 2010, well into writing this book, when I heard a teaser for the ten o'clock news saying, "Words were exchanged in anger today at a meeting between the mayors of Fargo and Moorhead, the Army Corps of Engineers and other officials trying to sort out the best course of action for long-term flood control."

When the news came on at ten, I was there, seated firmly in front of the television. I wasn't going to miss a syllable. *I've lived here five years and I'm finally going to see a political dust-up!* I was breathless with anticipation.

The story's going to video! The anchor handed over to someone who was "there today." *I'm actually going to get to see this!*

The video came on. *It's Fargo Mayor Dennis Walaker! The hero of the floods!* He looked a little more awake than usual – he's always wide awake, I've learned, but he's just so laid back he usually doesn't quite look it – so I waited for the outburst. The *words exchanged in anger*.

Mayor Walaker proceeded to make a very logical point about not agreeing to a certain course of action if it would overly narrow the city's options at a later date. He seemed slightly more intense than his usual fully-laid back self.

I waited for the *words exchanged in anger*. But suddenly, the anchorman was back onscreen again, saying, "So you can see, they exchanged some heated words today down at the City Commission offices..."

Wait a minute, I thought to myself. *That's it?* That's the *words exchanged in anger?*

I couldn't believe it, but they were onto the next story.

"That's not words exchanged in anger!" I said aloud to the television. "Where I come from, that's called someone making a valid point." I was getting louder. *"Words exchanged in anger my a**.* Where I've spent most of my years, rare is the occasion when anyone is quite that civil and sensible making a political point..."

"Who are you talking to?" My wife asked. My little rant had brought her out of our bedroom.

"Oh, the television anchor," I said.

"Okaaaayyy..." she said, raising her eyebrows. "You feeling okay, honey?"

I laughed. She smiled.

"It's time to get the kids into bed," she said.

Thinking about it later that night, I was still irritated. I thought the teaser had been misleading. But then, I realized, maybe seeing Mayor Walaker that intense qualified as *words exchanged in anger* around here.

And I started to chuckle.

*　　　*　　　*

Don't get me wrong. There are still differing political philosophies here. The Republicans still believe primarily in self-reliance.

So does just about everyone else in North Dakota. Never met a more self-reliant bunch. Those who aren't self-reliant move south or die young.

The Democrats still believe primarily in helping the other guy.

So does just about everyone else in North Dakota. Never met a more helpful bunch. Anyone who isn't helpful stands out like a sore thumb.

I guess those are two of the main reasons everybody's pretty happy around here. And maybe why, for the last fifty years, neither party has dominated. And why most of the folks who get elected in these parts tend to be pretty sensible, regardless of party. If you're too young to remember how Republicans and Democrats used to treat each other like human beings and work together to find sensible solutions a few decades back, just come to North Dakota and watch. If you want to see the kind of sane political competition *and cooperation* that got us out of the Great Depression, won World War II, created the healthiest 60-year stretch of economic growth in the history of the world and won the Cold War, it's still on display here.

North Dakota is the only state in the country where you're not required to register to vote. You don't have to declare yourself "with these guys" and "against those guys" before you can vote, as people are forced to in the other forty-nine states.

72

To be allowed to vote here, you only need to show that you're an American citizen living in North Dakota. *Gee, what a novel approach.*

North Dakota is full of self-reliant Democrats and help-the-other guy Republicans – as well as, of course, a healthy dose of independent Independents – and probably a whole bunch of people like me who really appreciate not being forced to declare themselves anything other than just *an American living in North Dakota.* Regardless of political affiliation, almost no one I've met here seems to take their own politics *too* seriously. Many often vote for someone on the other side of the aisle – mainly, I think, because people around here are still in touch with reality enough to know that competence usually trumps ideology, and that's as true for governors and senators as it is for plumbers and accountants.

But I still get the biggest kick out of candidates running for office who seem unable to say enough nice things about their opponents.

Well, I also have something nice I'd like to say, to North Dakotans of every political stripe:

How Fargo of You.

CHAPTER 7

The News from Fargo

Sometimes it takes a while to get it.

Watching the local television news in Fargo was a new kind of experience. It began innocently enough, during our first visit to Fargo when, one night, Charlene and I caught a teaser for the upcoming newscast. It went something like:

> *On their eightieth year in Fargo, the local Kiwanis Club has once again broken their annual fundraising record to benefit children! Stay tuned for details at ten!*

"Oh my goodness…" I remember saying to Charlene, slightly stunned, "That's their *top story!*"

"I know!" she replied, eyes wide. Then we broke out in laughter.

I seem to recall a couple of other "lead stories" we caught during our first visit:

Three teens detained in connection with the graffiti found outside the West Fargo High gym last week. Story at ten.

And:

The road construction on Main Avenue is a week behind schedule. Stay tuned at ten and hear what affected businesses have to say.

Every time we caught one of these teasers, we'd start laughing all over again.

In Arizona, we avoided the local news like the plague – because it *was* a plague, of sorts: Every evening, grisly murders, horrendous car wrecks celebrated with video from mind-jarring angles, crimes involving children.

We didn't want to hear about these things, and gained nothing by knowing them – except, perhaps, the knowledge that we'd rather be somewhere else. Now, the Fargo newscasts were showing us what somewhere else looked like – and all we could do was laugh!

I found myself feeling sorry for the local news people. I had friends back in Phoenix who were reporters, and I kept trying to picture how they'd react to a news beat where the most exciting thing happening in a 24-hour period was the capture of some fugitive teenagers who'd graffitied the outside of a local high school gym. My reporter friends – the ones who'd told me there were days when one or two of the more "unremarkable" homicides in Phoenix didn't make it into the paper or onto the local newscasts *at all* – complained about how crime-ridden Phoenix had become. But after a tiny taste of the Fargo news scene, I wondered if they wouldn't experience crime withdrawal symptoms if plopped into Fargo and told, "Here – Report *This*."

Then, on our second Saturday night in North Dakota – our last night staying with Melody – Charlene and I actually watched a full local newscast.

At first, I found it amusing. By the end, it was a revelation. Ultimately, it redefined local television journalism for me.

The newscast opened with a crime report about an overnight burglary in a small retail shop. We chuckled. Back in Phoenix, shopkeepers finding their places burgled overnight were a dime a dozen. They might have to make a second phone call to get a cop to show up, much less the local media. But this was Fargo's big crime for the day. Damage to the shop was minimal.

Then there was an update on a court case involving a murder that had taken place somewhere in North Dakota *the year before.* "Wow, honey," I said to Charlene, "It happened last year and they're *still talking about it.*"

"Yeah," she nodded, in her best *See what it's like here?* tone of voice.

The anchor lady was now saying something about a car accident involving minor injuries.

That was it for the bad news.

Most of the next ten minutes was filled with video from little festivals, concerts, street fairs and charity fundraisers going on that weekend, not just in Fargo, but in several little towns dozens of miles away.

This was a nostalgic experience for Charlene, reminding her of growing up in smaller towns in Wisconsin. For me, it was unlike anything I'd ever seen. *Wow, these guys are really desperate for news,* I thought to myself. But I kept silent. I was pretty sure Charlene would get mad at me if I said it out loud, disturbing her trip down memory lane.

I still wasn't getting it.

Then came the weather. In Phoenix, about 300 days out of the year, a typical weather report is just a slight variation on the classic George Carlin "hippy-dippy weather, man" routine:

Today, the sun was hot and the air was dry. The forecast for tomorrow is for more sun, also hot and dry. In between, the forecast is for dark cooling — but not a lot of darkness, because the city lights brighten the desert sky for about a hundred miles in every direction. And not much cooling, either, because there's so much concrete and asphalt now that the desert doesn't cool off at night like it used to...

Whenever Charlene, who's from the Midwest, would see me watching a weather report in Phoenix, she'd say, "That's not weather." Watching my first ten o'clock newscast in Fargo, I began to understand what she meant:

There may be some scattered rain tomorrow afternoon in the southeast corner of the state, perhaps ranging as far north as the Canadian border – the jet stream is kind of whipping things around right now, so we can't really pin things down more than that. But the temperature should make it into the eighties during the day, regardless of precipitation. At night, though, a cold snap will hit as an arctic front moves through, dropping temperatures fairly dramatically. The thermometer may even dip below freezing briefly, so gardeners and farmers may want to cover up or spray some mist around sunset to protect their plants...

"Jeez honey, it's July and tomorrow night it may go below freezing!" I said, incredulous, as the newscast went to commercial.

"Yeah, and it will be over eighty during the day," she replied. "That's *weather*. *Real* weather. See what I've been telling you all these years? You're finally experiencing some *real weather*."

Charlene got up from the couch where we were sitting. "I'll let you watch the sports," she said. "You can tell me if you learn anything exciting." She walked out to the kitchen and started chatting with Melody.

It was then, during the sportscast, that I finally started to *get* the Fargo news. But it didn't happen right away. For the next seven minutes or so, I was taken on a little mini-tour of half the sporting facilities in and around Fargo, the sportscaster regaling me with tales from the North Dakota minor league baseball team, the Redhawks, to an off-season high school track meet at Schlanser Track on the NDSU campus.

Sports is supposed to start out with the most important national sports events, I thought to myself. But this is just a lot of little local stuff. Any one of these stories would only be a ten-second tag at the end of a sportscast in Phoenix. Where's the big sports?

I got my answer after the tour of local sports facilities, learning that the Minnesota Twins had beaten the Tigers in Detroit that day, and something about a possible last-minute trade the Minnesota Vikings were considering before the start of pre-season. Those were the only mentions of anything that might possibly qualify as national sports stories – and they were only mentioned because they qualified, to some degree, as *local*.

It was completely topsy-turvy from what I was used to. The largest national and international sporting events of the day led the sportscasts in the places I'd lived. But in Fargo, they were completely ignored. On the other hand, a lot of little local sporting events, usually completely ignored by the "local" press where I'd lived, had been covered exhaustively.

And it finally started to slowly seep into my brain this might make great sense. After all, there were now dozens of channels on cable where you could learn more than everything you ever wanted to know about national and international sporting events. It began to dawn on me that the "local" sportscasts I was accustomed to weren't *local* at all. They were, for the most part, inexpensive, unoriginal regurgitations of stories available via dozens of other channels. I sat back in the couch as it struck me that the big-city sportscasts I was used to had become obsolete anachronisms, left over from the days when there weren't ten cable channels covering sports better than any local channel ever could.

And then it hit me: *I just witnessed the most time-and-work-intensive local sports broadcast **I've ever seen**.*

Only then did the big picture really begin coming into focus. *Everything I'd just watched had followed the same pattern* – the news and weather, as well as the sports, had all involved exhaustive local coverage. I hadn't just watched a low-budget version of a big-city newscast, as I'd been assuming. *I may have just witnessed the most exhaustive local news broadcast I've ever seen in my life,* I suddenly realized, stunned.

These people aren't obsessed with the "big" story, or they'd be regurgitating all the national news, weather and sports like the "local" newscasts in Phoenix do, and saving themselves a lot of time, money and effort in the process.

I was starting to "get" the Fargo news.

*Oh... it's all about **community**.* What a shock.

*　　　　　*　　　　　*

My next big step *getting* the Fargo news came four years later, as we were in the process of moving here. I was back in Arizona with the kids and my mom, selling our two places, while Charlene was busy in Fargo looking for our new house and a job. One day, I started thinking about the Fargo news again, and the tiny amount of crime reportage compared to Phoenix. I found myself wondering: *Just how much lower is the Fargo crime rate?*

Snooping around on the Internet, I found *there had only been one murder in Fargo in 2004.* That was pretty different from Phoenix, which occasionally had a half-dozen or so in single day.

But of course, Phoenix has many times the population of Fargo. And we didn't live in Phoenix, actually, but in Glendale, a suburb west of Phoenix. So I found a website for Glendale which showed there had been 18 murders in Glendale in 2004.[1] Conveniently, this website also showed that Glendale, with a

---

[1] Again, see notes on the chapters at the back of the book for details on this and other websites discussed here.

population of just under 240,000, therefore had a murder rate of 7.5 murders for every 100,000 people living in the city during 2004. I quickly returned to the Fargo site and saw that it also gave the Fargo murder rate for 2004 – 1.1 murders per 100,000 people living there, since Fargo had a population of just over 90,000 people in 2004.

Wow, so the Fargo murder rate is only about 1/7th that of Glendale, I thought to myself.

I thought about the basic laws of probability for a second. *That's almost the difference between the chances of flipping a coin once and getting heads, or flipping it **four times** and getting heads every time.*

But just as I was congratulating myself on our great good judgment in moving to Fargo, something else on the Fargo website caught my eye: *There were **no** murders in Fargo in 2001, 2002 or 2003!* So the murder rate in Fargo over the previous four years *was only one-fourth as high as I'd thought!* I quickly divided 1.1 by four and got .275 – just over ¼ of a homicide per year for every 100,000 in population. Then I went back to the Glendale website and calculated the average murder rate in Glendale 2001-2004: It was 7.05 murders per 100,000 in population. Dividing 7.05 by .275 showed me that *Fargo had less than 1/25th the murder rate of Glendale!*

So it's not our imagination, I thought. *It's the difference in the risk of driving from Phoenix to Fargo and base jumping off the edge of the Grand Canyon! No wonder we feel so much safer in Fargo.*

But I wondered. We lived less than a mile from the west edge of Phoenix. *To be fair, I should probably figure out the average murder rate for the Phoenix-Glendale region,* I thought. I soon found a website for Phoenix similar to the ones I'd used for Fargo and Glendale and quickly discovered *the Phoenix murder rate for 2001-2004 exceeded 15 murders per 100,000 in population, more than double the murder rate of Glendale!*

So Fargo has less than 1/50th *the murder rate of Phoenix,* I realized, completely stunned. *That's less than 2 percent!*

By this time I felt compelled to do a bunch of calculations to figure out the murder rate for the combined Phoenix-Glendale area: *It was 49 times higher than the murder rate for Fargo!*

I was on a roll. I found several lists of the ten most dangerous cities in the U.S. and *Phoenix wasn't on any of them!* There were apparently many more dangerous places you could live, if you wanted to.

Then I looked for lists of the safest places to live in America and *the Fargo-Moorhead region was near the top of every one.*

No wonder the Fargo news is so damn cheery, I thought to myself. *They hardly have anything else to report on.*

That was my second great experience *getting* the news from Fargo.

*   *   *

Having lived here for five years now, I can attest that our news isn't always light faire. There are, on very rare occasions, murders in North Dakota – and we get to hear about them over and over and over: When they happen. As the investigation progresses. When the perpetrators are apprehended. After the arrest is made. The blow-by-blow throughout the court proceedings. This goes on for months, sometimes years, on every single murder case. Fargo isn't like Phoenix or L.A., where some murders don't even rate a single sentence on local television, radio, or in the paper. Quite the opposite.

Because serious crime is rare in this part of the world, arrests are usually made quickly. Murders are so uncommon that just about every police professional – indeed, every member of the community who can – is likely to contribute to solving the crime. This kind of focused effort on every significant case makes a big difference. Suspects are usually arrested amazingly fast, with stunning amounts of lawfully gathered evidence compiled close to flawlessly. I've witnessed this same pattern via the news several times since moving here. I interpret it very simply: If a bunch of well-trained, well-rested detectives have all month to solve one major crime, things turn out a lot better than when one overworked, under-rested detective has several new crimes on his plate every week. Ergo, Fargo is no place for bad guys.

Our last big murder, about a year ago, is a case in point. It was, allegedly, a hired hit against a dentist who had just moved here, his murder directed out of Oklahoma, from where he'd recently moved. Despite the distances involved, arrests of the alleged hit man and the dentist's former father-in-law, accused of paying for the hit, took place in Oklahoma within two weeks of the killing. And of course, whenever there's even the slightest court action in the case, we hear all about it.

*   *   *

Without dozens of crime stories to chase day after day, local journalists end up doing what almost every other professional around here seems to do – spend a lot of time and effort helping the local community, and the world at large.

I learned this first-hand during our second spring in Fargo, when Melody invited us to a local fundraiser. She explained that a friend she worked with, Deanna Micheli, had founded a non-profit group a few years earlier dedicated to recycling used medical equipment and supplies. The name of her charity was HERO – Health Equipment Recycling Organization – and they make recon-ditioned, sometimes exorbitantly expensive medical equipment available to rural areas in North Dakota and northwest Minnesota – and more recently, to countries around the world, on every continent except Antarctica.

It all started when Deanna, a Registered Nurse, had become aware that expensive, perfectly usable medical materials and equipment were regularly thrown into landfills, as hospitals and other health facilities continuously upgraded to the latest technology. And she knew that these were the kinds of things that could save lives.

So she'd done something about it. And in Fargo, she'd found a lot of people willing to help. It was a great idea that could do a lot of people untold good. HERO was now thriving, with the slogan "Save a Life and Save the Earth," and their annual fundraiser was scheduled for the coming Friday at the Fargo Air Museum, Melody told us. It sounded great to Charlene and me, and we agreed to meet Melody and her boyfriend Paul at the event.

Wandering the Fargo Air Museum was a blast. It's filled with old planes in great condition and lots of history. Like most Fargo events, the dress was casual, similar to most everyone's demeanor. There's just not much put-on around here, no matter the occasion.

The MCs for the evening were Kerstin Kealy, co-anchor of the evening news for WDAY, the local ABC affiliate, along with WDAY reporter Kevin Wallevand, a HERO board member. The station, of course, was donating its services to the proceedings. Every thirty minutes or so, Kevin or Kerstin would regale us with one of the many fascinating stories from HERO's brief history.

Not long after we arrived, Charlene, Mel, Paul and I helped ourselves to some great food laid out along a wonderful buffet line, and spent about a half hour eating and chatting. But I was still a bit hungry – and some of the food had been exceptionally good. The buffet line was beckoning me back. I looked up. *No one in line!* "I'm going back to the now-empty buffet line," I said to Charlene. "Care to join me?"

"No thanks," she said. "Go for it." I went.

Things were about to get unexpectedly interesting.

I started at the third dish down the buffet line, some particularly delicious Swedish meatballs. There were only about a dozen left. My stomach thought about taking five or six, but my brain decided that would be very *unFargo* of me. I took three and moved on to the veggie appetizers.

About then, a woman I recognized as WDAY co-anchor Kerstin Kealy, who I'd never met, arrived at my right, also going for the Swedish meatballs. *I'm not the only one noticing the line is empty and eyeing those last few meatballs*, I thought to myself.

"Excuse me, Kerstin," came a plaintive voice from the other side of the buffet table. I looked up. A middle-aged lady was approaching adoringly from the other side of the buffet line, sort of bent over like she was bowing to a queen. "I know you don't like to be bothered, but..."

"Oh, no, that's fine," Kerstin smiled back, trying her best to put the woman at ease, meatball tongs pausing mid-swoop. She immediately gave the woman her full attention.

"Well, I'm really *sorry*," the woman persisted, all doe-eyed, "I know you don't like to be bothered..." Like many people, this lady was clearly uncomfortable talking to someone she only knew from television.

"No, *really*," Kerstin insisted, in the cheeriest voice imaginable, "it's *okay*." She was nodding to the woman with a big smile, encouraging her to speak. Plate poised in her left hand. Tongs hovering in midair over the meatballs in her right. Her complete, undivided attention was now on the woman across the buffet table from her. It was a magnificent attempt to relax the very nervous lady.

No such luck. The woman stammered, "Well, uh, you know…" Her cheeks were starting to turn pink. I was fully absorbed in the moment now, trying not to be obvious, still picking at the veggies. There was no one within twenty feet of the three of us. The air began crackling with tension as it became unclear whether the woman would actually be able to say what she had on her mind. "…I just adore you, I watch you every night…"

Kirsten was nodding, "Thank you," she said, big smile glowing, tongs still hovering. The tension began to subside.

"…but I *know* you don't, uh…*like to be…*" the lady again returned to a halting, propitiative tone, and it once more became unclear whether she'd ever relax enough to actually express whatever it was she'd originally come over to say. Though I appeared an innocent bystander, I was still less than a foot from Kerstin, unable to pull myself away from the grisly scene unfolding across the buffet line before me. The tension was now skyrocketing to unmanageable levels. I began to wonder if Kerstin would be stuck there all night trying to put this woman at ease.

Suddenly an idea hit me. It might work. If I struck at just...
the... right... moment...

"...I *know* you don't, uh... like to be *bothered*..." the woman
was now saying again, for the third time.

"No, really, she *does*," I said as offhandedly as possible,
looking directly at the nervous lady, "you know, she was just
telling me, *not a minute ago,* 'You know, I really wish someone
would come over here and *bother* me'..."

The lady was now looking at me slack-jawed, half-stunned.
And then suddenly, a little smile began to break across her face.

At the same time, Kerstin erupted with laughter to my
right. I was still looking at the lady, working my most charming
smile, encouraging her to play along. Then I heard Kerstin catch
herself, stifling her sudden outburst. I turned my head to look at
Kerstin just in time to catch a quickly suppressed smile, eyes
furiously boring holes into mine for having made her laugh
when she least wanted to. "Oh!!!" was all she said, furrowing
her brow.

Then suddenly, I was flying to my left! I had to catch my
footing quickly to avoid spilling my Swedish meatballs. *What
just happened?* I wondered for a split second. One moment,
Kirsten was holding a plate in one hand and tongs in the other,
and the next, I was a human pinball. Was this Anchorwoman
some kind of Jedi master?

Then a dull ache in my right hip told me – I'd just been very
thoroughly *bumped!*

As I regained my footing and composure, I looked back and saw the two ladies now happily chatting away across the buffet line from each other as if nothing had happened – and I was happily a few feet away from Kerstin's deadly left hip. They were both relaxing into a friendly conversation. *I need to get out of here*, I thought, trying to refocus on the buffet line before me. I limped down the line and back to our table.

Hey, at least I'm still alive, I thought to myself.

Charity comes in all forms around here.

*   *   *

Well, that's how I *got* the news from Fargo. And whenever I listen to Kerstin delivering it, I almost always, with a slight twinge in my right hip, find myself thinking...

How Fargo of You.

CHAPTER 8

The Hunter Cafe

Forget your cash, find the hidden treasure.

It all started with a little Styrofoam container hastily marked *"Rhub,"* in green marker.

"Excuse me, but does that stand for *rhubarb*?" I asked the friendly-looking blonde lady in the administrative office of my son's new school. I was pointing at the container sitting on her desk.

"Yes, it's rhubarb pie," she answered with a friendly, if slightly bewildered, smile.

"Is it *real* rhubarb, not mixed with anything else, like strawberry or something?" I was afraid it was too good to be true.

A light of recognition came to her eyes. "Oh, yes. It's from the Hunter Cafe. I know what you mean about store-bought 'strawberry rhubarb' pies where you can't taste any rhubarb. The lady who owns the Hunter Cafe grows the rhubarb right in her own garden!"

My mouth was starting to water. I couldn't believe my good luck – I'd never had fresh-from-the-garden rhubarb pie!

But I had no idea where the Hunter Cafe was. Suddenly, I noticed the sign above the nice blonde lady's desk with her name on it.

"I'm sorry, Carrie – you're Carrie, right?"

"Yeah," she said in her very friendly voice.

"I'm sorry, Carrie, but I have no idea where the Hunter Cafe is."

"Well, you head west," Carrie said, pointing, "until you get to the first stop sign. Then turn right, and it's just a couple of miles or so up the road from there."

"About how far west is the first stop sign, where I turn right?"

"Oh, *about six miles or so.*" Carrie said this in a perfectly normal tone of voice. I've just added the emphasis because that's how I heard it.

I suppose I should explain I was at Northern Cass, a large, spacious, beautiful, modern K-12 school springing out of the middle of the prairie, with nothing for miles in any direction but fields divided here and there by long stands of trees and an occasional farmhouse. It's named for the simple fact that it sits at the northern end of Cass County, of which Fargo is the county seat. Walking through the front doors of this monolithic testament to the importance of children around here, you'll find the most relaxed, friendly, family-like atmosphere you've ever experienced inside a school, where staff and students of all ages happily interact in the uncrowded hallways, cafeteria and other common facilities. Watching the easy way people move with each other inside Northern Cass sometimes reminds me of the way breezy summer wheat moves in the fields that surround the place.

You'll see older kids with laptops and wireless access provided, younger children playing happily in a beautiful, modern playground, everything new or nearly new, from science labs to art equipment to the gym, along with a full football field, track facility, concession building and bleachers in back. Just to the west of the campus runs a beautiful, sizeable stand of large trees, where an array of wildlife, from eagles to squirrels, make their homes. Sometimes you'll see science classes out there on ecological excursions.

When you walk completely around the perimeter of the campus, looking outward in every direction, you can only make out about a half-dozen farm buildings, half of them miles off in the distance. These are interspersed with about twelve large stands of trees, near and far, each a mini-ecosystem like the little forest next to the campus. In the front of the school's parking lot, County Road 26 runs east-west, heading toward the horizon in both directions. County Road 26 is the only way in or out of the place that doesn't involve an all-terrain vehicle, a snowmobile or a helicopter, so I knew that was the road Carrie had just told me I would find a stop sign on, six miles to the west, en route to what I hoped would be rhubarb heaven.

But before I get back to my quest for pie, I should add this: At its core, Northern Cass boasts a highly dedicated teaching staff working with an average class size of about twenty students. So when we learned we had the option of sending our kids to Northern Cass – bus service *included*, even though the campus is located nearly twenty-five miles northwest of where we live, in Reiles Acres – we jumped at the opportunity to send Austen. He was just finishing fifth grade at Harwood Elementary, about two miles north of Reiles Acres. Harwood Elementary had been one of less than a hundred schools in the country to win a *No Child Left Behind* Blue Ribbon just that year, and Austen had loved Harwood since beginning third grade there three years earlier, a few days after we moved to North Dakota. So wherever Austen was to begin sixth grade, that school had some pretty big shoes to fill.

About five minutes into our first tour of Northern Cass, we were enthralled. We couldn't have imagined a more wonderful school for Austen to go through – and grow through – his adolescence. It was, in some ways, even beyond our wildest dreams.

Don't get me wrong, the schools in nearby West Fargo, just a few miles south of our home in Reiles Acres, which were also available to Austen, are all a cut above the vast majority of schools in the rest of the country. But when we visited Northern Cass, it seemed in a class utterly by itself. Northern Cass is another North Dakota treasure hidden in plain view, as so many are.

That's why we were there that day, enrolling Austen – and why, once his older sister Anastasia had visited a few times during Austen's first year there, she chose to start her freshman year of high school at Northern Cass.

"So the nearest stop sign," I asked Carrie, "is six miles down the road?"

Carrie looked at one of her co-workers, who'd overheard our conversation. After looking at each other for a half-second or so, they both nodded. "Yeah," she said.

"Mmm-hmm." Confirmed her coworker, still nodding.

I couldn't help but smile. I was reminded of a large framed photograph we have hanging above our fireplace, taken by a renowned local photographer, Wayne Gudmundson. It shows a North Dakota road heading off into the far-distant horizon. Gently rolling prairie spreads out from the road in every direction, a small, old farmhouse off to one side in the distance. Along the bottom of the photograph are the words *LIFE IN THE VAST LANE*, with Wayne's signature just beneath them.

"And after I turn right, about how far is it before I reach the Hunter Cafe?"

"Oh, once you turn, Hunter's just a couple miles or so down the road," Carrie said.

"You mean the cafe?"

"Well, it's there, in the middle of town."

"Oh, you mean Hunter's a *town*."

"*Yeah*," Carrie said, with a wry smile and a *hey, you catch on quick* kind of look.

"Mmmm... so the *Hunter Cafe* is in the town of *Hunter*," I said in my best Sherlock Holmes, wagging my finger, "I bet that's *why* it's called the *Hunter Cafe*."

Carrie chuckled. "You got it."

"Well, I didn't know there even was a town around here called Hunter," I tried to explain, "so I just figured the Hunter Cafe featured locally hunted wild boar or something."

Carrie and her co-workers laughed.

"Our meeting's starting," Charlene said, tugging at my sleeve, then heading down the hall toward the conference room. I followed.

"Thanks for the directions, Carrie." I said, looking back. "I'll tell them you sent me."

"You'll *love* it!"

Much to my disappointment, after we enrolled Austen that day, we didn't have time to just "head up" to Hunter – which, from the school, is in exactly opposite direction as our home in Reiles' Acres.

But a few weeks later, the next time I had a good excuse to visit Northern Cass, I made a point of leaving an extra half-hour early so I could drop into the Hunter Cafe. So after driving 25 miles across the prairie to reach the school, I just kept heading west on County Road 26, right past the campus. Six miles down the road, out in the middle of nowhere – not a building in any direction for as far as the eye could see, except some grain silos off to the north – there was the stop sign, just as Carrie had said. I turned right, and about two miles up the road I came to the little farming town of Hunter, built around the silos I'd seen from the stop sign. The silos looked ten stories high or so, on the left side of the road, next to the railroad tracks. As I neared them, about the middle of town, I spotted a small, attractive sign for the Hunter Cafe, across from the silos. I pulled into the parking lot and went inside.

It was a bit like walking through a time portal, back to the 1950s – not the flashy 1950s so often contrived in modern media, but the more subdued, real 1950s of my early youth. A few customers were sitting on comfortably padded metal-legged chairs around square Formica tables, while others were ensconced in light green Naugahyde booths with Formica tabletops, sipping coffee and eating what looked like truly home-cooked food. There was also a small, curved, old-style fountain bar with a faux-marble top and classic, round, backless chrome-and-red-leather stools. It was clean and simple.

And the array of aromas was *delicious*.

"May I help you?" A friendly-looking middle-aged lady behind the cash register had noticed I was just standing inside the front door, looking around.

"Yes, you *can*," I said, walking over toward the counter. "I heard you have *great* pies. I was hoping to get some rhubarb."

"I'm sorry," she said sympathetically, "we're all out of rhubarb. It's usually gone by this time."

I was surprised. It was only 3:45 in the afternoon. The surprise must have shown on my face, so the nice lady, who of course knew I wasn't a regular – anyone who spends any time in Hunter, after all, knows everyone else who spends any time in Hunter – decided to enlighten me: "We close in fifteen minutes."

They close at four on weekdays! I thought to myself. Then it occurred to me: *The Hunter schedule operates around people, not the other way around.*

"Oh… shucks. I was really looking forward to some home-grown rhubarb," I said, "which I've never had. I heard you folks grow your own rhubarb."

"Yes, Deb does," the lady said with a smile. "If you call ahead, she'll bake one and hold it for you." She handed me an attractive business card that read *Hunter Cafe & Bakery, (701) 874-BAKE,* and beneath that: *Jim, Deb, Mathew Tarvestad.*

"Thanks, I'll definitely call ahead the next time I'm coming out this way," I said, putting the card in my pocket. "But since I'm here, do you have any kind of pie left?"

"We still have a couple pieces of sour cream and raisin. That's about it."

"Sour cream and raisin?" I asked. I'd never heard of such a combination. It sounded awful, but I had trouble imagining

100

these people baking anything awful. "Okay, I'll try a piece to go."

That night, after dinner, Charlene, my mom and I shared our lone piece of sour cream and raisin pie. It was a slice of heaven.

Man, what's the rhubarb going to be like? I wondered. Then I remembered the smells. *What's the rest of their food like?*

I knew I'd discovered another hidden-out-in-the-open North Dakota treasure. But I hadn't the faintest clue how deep it went. Yet.

*   *   *

About a month or so after our first tiny taste of the Hunter Cafe, Austen came home with a notice that his sixth grade music class would be putting on a recital after school the next week. I immediately made a note to myself, and the next morning, I called the Hunter Cafe.

"Hunter Cafe, this is Deb," came a cheerful voice from the other end.

"I bet you're the lady who owns the place and bakes the pies?"

"That's me!"

"I heard you grow your own rhubarb."

"Yes I do!"

"I *have to have* one of your rhubarb pies. I've never had a pie made with rhubarb fresh from the garden. And I'd like a sour cream and raisin pie, too, please. I brought home a piece from your place just to try a while back, and it was *amazing*. Did you come up with that recipe yourself?"

"You mean the sour cream and raisin?"

"Yes. We'd never had it, or even heard of it before."

Oh, no, that's an *old* recipe, from somewhere around here a hundred years ago or so, I think, when fresh fruit was hard to come by for about half the year. I'm glad you enjoyed it."

"That's a severe understatement."

Deb laughed. "Well, thank you!" She said, still chuckling. "When would you like your two pies?"

"Let's see..." I glanced at my calendar. "My son's recital at Northern Cass is next Wednesday, so I'll be coming by then."

"Okay. They'll be ready by noon!"

"Oh, Deb," I said, suddenly remembering an important detail. "How late are you open on Wednesday?"

"Wednesday is our late day," Deb said, "so we're open 'til seven."

"Fantastic! We'll just stop by after the recital."

"Great! Feel free to have dinner with us after the recital."

"You know, that's a good idea. We might do that."

*   *   *

That night, I told Charlene about my conversation with Deb. "So what do you think, honey, should we have dinner at the Hunter Cafe after Austen's recital?"

"That sounds *great*," she said, "but let me check the schedule – I think Anastasia might have skating that night."

Our daughter is a fairly dedicated figure skater. She had an out-of-town competition coming up soon, and her practice schedule was pretty intense. "Let's see," Charlene said, looking through her skating papers. "You said Austen's recital starts at four-thirty?"

"Yeah."

Charlene's face suddenly took on a look of disappointment. "Oh, no... Anastasia's got an important practice at six that night, with a professional from out of town. Austen's recital will last until *at least* five-thirty. We'll never be able to make it in time from Northern Cass."

It's a good 35-mile drive from Northern Cass to the Moorhead Sports Center, where Anastasia skates, in Moorhead, Minnesota – Fargo's sister city just across the Red River. Short of renting a helicopter, there was no way we'd ever get Anastasia from Austen's recital to her practice session on time. Even wonderful things, like Northern Cass, sometimes have their drawbacks.

"Well..." I began to rearrange my ideas. Suddenly, Charlene's face brightened.

"Why don't you and Austen have a boy's night out?" She spoke in the cheery voice that comes whenever she turns lemons into lemonade.

"That's what I was starting to think," I said. (Hey, I was getting there.)

"You go to the recital, and afterwards, you and Austen have dinner at the Hunter Cafe."

"That sounds *great!*" It would be a blast. Austen's a very funny kid – especially if you're a guy with a less than fully matured sense of humor and his more demure mother and older sister aren't there to get grossed out every few minutes. And he *loves* good food.

"But *be sure to bring enough cash with you,*" Charlene 's tone turned suddenly serious.

I looked at her blankly. I had no idea why she was giving me these instructions. But her intensity meant only one thing: It must be *important.*

"Why do I need cash?" I asked.

"Look, honey, you're addicted to your debit card, but a lot of these little towns don't take cards. You have to bring enough cash with you to pay for dinner and the pies and whatever else you're going to get. Or bring your checkbook, but you can't be certain they'll take checks. Better yet, bring your checkbook *and* cash."

I had no idea how she knew this. I'd spent more time on the road in North Dakota and Minnesota on short business trips since we'd moved here than Charlene, but hadn't noticed that small towns sometimes didn't take cards. I always carry plenty of cash on business trips, though, so maybe I just hadn't noticed when cash was my only option. I'll tell you one thing, though: I didn't doubt my wife. She *knows* things.

*   *   *

The day of the recital, I left home about four, a half-hour before the event was scheduled to begin. Austen was still at school, in final rehearsal. I wouldn't see him until he was onstage with the other sixth graders.

A little over a mile from our house, I got on I-29 and headed north. A couple of miles further down the road, I passed the small town of Harwood, where both Anastasia and Austen had attended elementary school after we moved here. The kids, Charlene and I had made a lot of friends there. A wave of wonderful memories swept over me as the town flew by. Soon, nothing but flat prairie lay before me, as far as the eye could see. About fifteen miles up the Interstate, I took the exit marked *Gardner*, for a very small town I have yet to see, because it's hidden behind a stand of trees on the east side of the freeway, while Northern Cass is to the west. I turned left, heading west toward the school, into the lowering sun. More endless prairie all around. Only one other car was visible in the distance, about a mile or so ahead, heading the same direction I was. *Probably going to the recital*, I thought. About five minutes later, I could begin to make out the school a couple of miles ahead, barely visible in front of the sizeable stand of tall trees behind it, now in silhouette, the sun setting behind it. It was beautiful.

As I watched the car a mile or so ahead pull into the school parking lot, I realized how much I was anticipating our *boys night out*. If you had told me in my twenties I would feel this way about such simple things, in such a simple place, I would have told you you were crazy. But now, I know better. It's that guy in his twenties who was missing out.

I enjoyed the recital, and found Austen immediately afterwards. "That was great, Austen," I told him. "I actually heard your voice a few times above the others. You sounded good."

"Thanks, dad," he said, unenthusiastically. Austen can sing well, but in sixth grade he feigned disinterest. It wasn't cool, I guess.

"You ready to go to the Hunter Cafe?" I asked. Charlene and I had already discussed *boys night out* with him.

"Yeah, I'm really hungry!" he said, brightening up. "Let me grab my backpack and coat." We were out of there in a flash.

We arrived at the Hunter Cafe a few minutes after six and took a booth. About half of the dozen-or-so tables and booths in the place were occupied. A cute, teenage waitress/hostess – apparently the only person working besides the cook – took our order. I asked for the meatloaf dinner, while Austen ordered the fried chicken. Before she left, I asked our waitress if she'd gone to school around here.

"I'm a senior at Northern Cass," she said.

"Really? Austen just started there this year," I said. "We just came from his sixth grade music recital there earlier tonight."

"Neat!" she said with a big grin. "Nice to meet you, Austen."

"Nice to meet you, too" Austen replied, a bit sheepishly. She nodded with a smile and swept off with our menus and order.

Our meals arrived about ten minutes later. Looking at my meatloaf dinner – complete with mixed vegetables and homemade mashed potatoes – reminded me of the meatloaf dinners my mother had fed me growing up. I looked over and saw Austen's plate filled with nearly half a bird! He took one bite and his eyes widened. His mouth still full, he exclaimed in a muffled – but fairly quiet, I'm proud to say – voice: "Wow! This is the best chicken I've ever tasted!" Austen is a connoisseur of all things meat. He's also more than willing to refuse anything he doesn't like, especially from someplace he's never been. I knew that chicken had to be *great*. As was my meatloaf, I was now learning, with my first bite.

A minute later, as our waitress passed by with her hands free for the moment, I stopped her. "Excuse me," I said, "but do you know where this chicken came from?"

She gave me a puzzled look and started to point toward the kitchen. "Well, we fix our own..."

I suddenly realized she was probably about to tell me it came from the kitchen of the Hunter Cafe, which was the correct answer to the question I'd asked. I interrupted: "No, I mean, where do you folks, here at the cafe, get your chicken?"

"Oh," She looked relieved, as if she'd just discovered I wasn't crazy after all. "I don't know, someplace around here."

"Like someplace with real chickens, walking around and stuff," I said, with a slight smile.

Nodding, she smiled back a little, but her face began to take on a *what other kind of chickens are there?* sort of look, no longer certain I wasn't so crazy after all.

"I mean like it was probably walking around yesterday, someplace a couple of miles or so from here, eating off the ground, with other chickens and everything."

She was exceedingly nice, unlike the haughty teenagers I'd grown used to dealing with in restaurants and other service establishments in Arizona, California and Florida. Nevertheless, I could tell she was completely mystified, earnestly wondering why I was interrogating her about where Austen's dinner had been yesterday and what it had been doing. She clearly didn't know that most of the chickens in America today hardly get to move a muscle for most of their lives, stuck in tiny single-bird coops, conveyor-belt feeders right under their beaks bringing by an almost continual stream of manufactured meal with antibiotics and other stuff to fatten them for market in the shortest possible time, nature be damned. The only kind of chickens she knew of, or had eaten for most of her life, were like the one Austen was now demolishing: A real, home-grown, happily running-around-loose-on-the-farm chicken from Hunter.

Nonetheless, I thought I'd give it one more try: "You know, a free-range chicken."

She kept smiling and nodding so at least I wouldn't feel so bad I was crazy after all, as she took a step toward another table – any other table. I nodded, letting her know she could go. Her ignorance of the corruption of the world beyond Hunter simply added to the wonder of the place for me. After all, why did she need to know how crazy the world out there had gotten, at least *yet*?

"That's all you'll ever get here," said a friendly lady perched with three very cute kids at the old-style fountain bar a few feet from us. "She's probably never heard of a free-range chicken, because you don't need a special name for it when it's the only kind you have."

I nodded, my mouth full of meatloaf. This woman and her kids had arrived at the cafe just after Austen and me. As she'd hoisted her very cheerful, well-behaved children up onto the bar stools, she'd recognized Austen from the music recital, which they'd also just attended, and immediately complimented him on his singing. To my delight, he'd given her a much more upbeat "Thanks" than he'd given me earlier. So we'd chatted a little before our meals arrived.

I was now grateful she was there. At least someone besides Austen knew I wasn't completely nuts talking about perfectly normal chickens as if they were diamonds dressed in feathers. Not that Austen had heard a word of my conversation with the waitress. He was still *hyperfocused* on devouring the subject of our discussion.

Suddenly, alarm shot through me. For the first time that day, I remembered Charlene's admonition: *Be sure to bring enough cash.* I put my fork down, pulled out my wallet and looked inside. Three dollars. I checked my pockets. I didn't have my checkbook with me.

There was still hope. Maybe Charlene's warning had been wrong, at least about the Hunter Cafe. If you're familiar with my wife, you know that hoping she's wrong is a desperately tiny thread to cling to. But it was all I had.

I spotted our waitress. I raised my hand. She was so nice she was incapable of ignoring me. Heading over, she began smiling and nodding at me, Mr. Crazy Person After All, before she even reached our table.

"Excuse me, but do you take cards?" I asked, showing her my Visa.

"No, just cash or checks." Her head went from nodding to shaking. Smile still firmly in place, friendly as possible.

"Oh, okay. Um… is there an ATM in town?"

"A what?" The bewildered look began coming back. *Crazy after all*, I could see her thinking, trying to hide it as she might.

"An ATM, an automatic teller machine, you know, where you can get money when the bank's closed?"

"Umm... maybe there's one in the bank, but they're closed now." I had her a little flustered at this point. It wasn't the effect I was going for. It's just a knack.

"Okay, but don't they have a little lobby in front of the bank that stays open, where you can make a deposit after hours?" That's where I was hoping to find an ATM.

"Umm... I don't know..." Her smile looked strained now, and her head was sort of bobbing around, not sure whether to nod or shake, as she started to take a step, once again, away from our table. *Must... Escape...* I could practically hear her thinking as I looked into her eyes.

"Okay, well... Can you just tell me where the bank is?" A look of relief came over her. *Finally, a question I can answer,* her thoughts spoke, *and after that he might **let me go.***

"It's right around the corner, the same building we're in," she said in her still, somehow, sweet voice.

"Alright, thank you very much," I said, relieved I didn't have to torture her any longer. She headed for other parts of the cafe. Any other parts. Quickly.

Despite my efforts to be quiet about my dilemma, the friendly lady with the three small children at the fountain bar had overheard my latest exchange with the waitress, and once again came to my rescue. "You'll probably have to go down to Arthur," she said quietly, trying to be discreet. "There's an ATM *there.*"

"I've been through Arthur once before," I said, "on a fishing trip with my son's Cub Scout den a couple of years ago. But I don't remember... where exactly is it from here?"

"Arthur's just six miles straight down the road from here," the nice lady said, pointing south.

There's only one road through Hunter, the one we'd turned north onto at the stop sign in the middle of nowhere. I just had to get back on it and head south, about four miles past the stop sign in the middle of nowhere, to get to Arthur.

"Are you sure the bank here in Hunter doesn't have an ATM?" I asked the lady.

"I kind of doubt it. But you can check."

"I'll do that right now. Thanks."

I looked at Austen. He was still in chicken reverie. I couldn't imagine a safer place in the universe to leave him. Literally. "Hey, Austen," I said, nudging his forearm.

"Yeah, dad?" He looked up at me, grudgingly breaking his communion with the bird from Hunter.

"I've got to walk around the corner to see if I can get a little cash from the local bank. I'll be back in a minute, okay?"

"Sure, dad." He went back to giving what was left of the bird his undivided attention.

I got up from the booth and walked outside. Around the corner I found the bank, just as the waitress had said, in the same building as the cafe, on the opposite side. There was a tiny glass-walled lobby, but the door to it was locked. A quick glance around the interior revealed there wasn't an ATM inside, anyway. I walked back to the restaurant and returned to our booth, where my last few bites of meatloaf were still waiting. I decided to eat them while I pondered our financial predicament.

The helpful lady with the three small children asked, "Any luck?"

I shook my head and swallowed. "No, no ATM." I looked at the clock on the wall and took my second-to-last bite. It was 6:30. In half an hour the cafe would close, and I had two dinners and two pies to pay for. I looked at Austen as I scooped the last morsel of home-cooked meatloaf off my plate. It had been little more than ten minutes since our dinners first arrived, and he still had a piece and a half of the former bird from Hunter left. He seemed just as enthralled as he'd been after the first bite.

"Well," I said to the helpful lady at the fountain bar as I polished off my meatloaf, "this is probably the safest place on the planet to leave my son for a few minutes while I go get some money."

"You might just as well leave him in your living room with a half-dozen aunts and uncles," she said with a chuckle.

"Hey, Austen," I said, nudging his forearm again. "I've got to go a few miles down the road to get some money from the nearest ATM. Do you just want me to leave you here to finish your chicken while I do that?"

"Mm-hmm." He glanced up and nodded emphatically. He wholeheartedly approved of the plan.

I got up once again, explained to our poor waitress what I was doing now, and asked if it was okay with her if I let Austen finish his dinner in the booth alone while I drove down to Arthur. She, of course, smiled and nodded kindly at Mr. Crazy Person After All.

I took off. It was now 6:35. I figured I had just enough time, if nothing went wrong, to get back about ten minutes before seven, when the Hunter Cafe would close its doors. I headed south on the only road out of Hunter, back out into the open prairie, then past the stop sign in the middle of nowhere. About four miles further, I came to the small farming town of Arthur. I looked for the gas station, where the nice lady with three cute kids had told me I'd find an ATM. Sure enough, there it was. I withdrew a hundred bucks and headed back up the road to Hunter.

When I returned to our booth, Austen was just picking the last few strands of chicken off of the pile of bones on his plate. "Hey dad," he said as I scooted into the booth, his typical greeting, a cool version of "hi". As an after-thought, he asked, "Did you get some money?"

"Yeah. We're all set."

With that, Austen looked very content.

I looked around. The clock read 6:53. The nice lady and her three cute kids were gone now, as were all the other customers except for one couple, a tall, slender man and woman about my age sitting in a corner booth. They'd been there, three booths down, when Austen and I had first arrived. Just then they got up to leave, paid the waitress at the cash register and walked

114

outside. Austen and I now had the place to ourselves. It was three minutes to seven.

"Well, we'd better collect our pies and go home," I said. It had been an eventful boys night out – music show, great food *and* an adventure. We'd made it, though. It was over. Or so I thought.

The waitress, brave soul that she was, ventured back to our table and started collecting our plates. They were scraped clean except for the bones of a Hunter chicken that had lived a good life and now found its purpose for being. "Can we get our check?" I asked.

"Um, your dinner's already been paid for," she said.

"Are you kidding?" I asked, stunned.

"No," she said, smiling and shaking her head.

"By whom? You guys?"

"No," she said, still smiling as she turned and walked back toward the kitchen with our dishes.

"Dad," Austen said, "you mean somebody else paid for us?"

"I guess so," I replied as Austen and I scooted out of the booth.

"Who was it?"

"I don't know yet."

"Wow. So you didn't have to go out for money after all?"

"Well, yes I did, Austen," I explained as we walked toward the front counter, "because we still have two pies to pay for." Then I wondered. "Say," I looked at our waitress, now behind the cash register, "whoever paid for our dinner didn't know we had pies on order and pay for them, too, did they?"

"No..." She glanced at a big paper bag by the register, which I noticed for the first time as she looked at it. I saw it had my name written on it in green marker. Looking at it, she asked, "Are you Marc?"

"I am," I answered. "Is there a rhubarb pie and a sour cream and raisin in there?" I asked, nodding toward the bag.

She looked inside and pulled out a little invoice. "Mm-hmm... yes." She smiled and looked at me. The crazy-person-after-all look seemed to be leaving her eyes just a little.

"How much do I owe you?"

"It comes to twenty-one eighty six," she said.

"So one of your other customers paid for our dinner?" I asked, handing her a couple of twenties.

"Mm-hmm," she said, nodding. But she wasn't offering to tell me more.

"Was it the lady with the three small children sitting at the bar?" She was the obvious choice. She'd understood my situation, our kids went to the same school, and she'd been gone by the time I'd returned from the money run.

"No, it wasn't her." The waitress said, smiling and shaking her head as she made my change.

I was even more stunned. That meant someone I'd never met, never even spoken with, had paid for dinner for Austen and me.

"Who was it, then?"

"I'm not supposed to say." She handed me my change.

I don't remember how I got it out of her, other than I knew I could, if I just kept at it. I'd already inadvertently put that sweet girl through the wringer a couple of times that night with questions, and I knew it wouldn't be long before she broke. It took maybe fifteen seconds of friendly questioning before she fessed up: "Well, it was the couple who were sitting in the corner booth."

"You mean the last ones to leave, the tall, slender middle-aged couple?"

"Yeah," she smiled and nodded.

I looked out into the parking lot. They were gone. "Who were they?" I asked.

She shrugged. "They come in once in a while."

"Did they say *why* they wanted to pay for our dinner?"

She shook her head.

"I suppose they wanted to leave a good impression of Hunter with the city guy who doesn't know enough to carry a little real money with him?"

She shrugged again and smiled a little. She looked at me and a sparkle flickered in her eye. *Maybe not crazy after all. Just different.* About this time, I realized there had been nothing forcing her to tell me about the couple paying for our dinners. *Nothing.* She could easily have kept her mouth shut and pocketed an extra twenty bucks or so. I looked at her again.

Something told me the thought to do something like that would never occur to her. It wasn't for any want of intelligence, just as our failures to connect earlier in the evening weren't due to any lack of intelligence on either her part or mine. These things stemmed from the fact that she lived in a different world than the one I'd been immersed in trying to comprehend most of my life. It was a world where chickens weren't corporate instruments to be manipulated to maximize profits, they were animals that ran around on farms with other animals, living chicken lives, and then they fed people good food. In her world, money was something you handed another person in exchange for something; it wasn't a bunch of anonymous blips between impersonal banking computers half a world away. Her world, the world of Hunter, was a world where a local couple would buy dinner for a man and his son whom they'd never met, who clearly didn't know how things were done around here, perhaps just so they might begin to understand.

I was beginning to understand. I was both exhilarated and dazed.

"Hmm. Well. How *Fargo* of them – *and* you." I said.

The bewildered look began returning to her face. *God knows I've already put this poor girl through too much unexplained commentary for one night,* I thought to myself. "It's just something I say about all the nice things people do for each other around here. I suppose in this case I ought to say how *Hunter* of them – and how Hunter of *you,* too, for… well, for putting up with me."

She let out a giggle, bringing a smile to my face. "Sure. Anytime," she said. I decided she was quite remarkable – not just in her honesty, or her obvious competence at handling the entire front end of the cafe completely on her own, but also in her tolerance for what must have appeared to her to be a very eccentric man. I left a five on the counter.

"Thanks!" she said, grinning ear to ear, a twinkle in her eye. *Yeah, a little crazy. But a nice crazy.*

"No – thank *you*," I said, still grinning at her big grin as Austen and I turned and left the Hunter Cafe.

*   *   *

The pies were *unbelievable.* And over the next few days, whenever I would get one out, cut a piece, and savor a bite, I couldn't help but think of the little town of Hunter, just past the stop sign in the middle of nowhere, and Deb, with her home-grown garden and cafe. Then I'd think of Carrie tolerating all my intrusive questions about the little Styrofoam container on her desk, and helping me along in my quest for pie. That reminded me of other people at Austen's new school, and how lucky we were to have them – there are undoubtedly billionaires in the world whose children have less, because you simply can't buy a sincere environment – you either have it or you don't. Then I'd think of the lady at the fountain bar with her three very cute kids from Northern Cass, the lady who'd always found just the right moment to say just the right thing to assuage my latest embarrassment, even when I pretended not to care. And, of course, I'd think of our cute, competent hostess/waitress and the great couple we'd never met who had anonymously bought us dinner. They'd all made the experience so much sweeter than any pie, no matter how delicious. And whenever I would think of them, and all they'd done out of a remarkably unselfconscious sense of kindness, I'd get a little misty-eyed, as I am right now, writing this.

And of course, you already know the phrase that kept running through my mind.

How Fargo of You.

CHAPTER 9

A Very Fargo Cab Ride

Discovering a different destination.

When I called the cab company that morning to book my first Fargo cab ride, I had no idea it was soon to change the direction of my life.

It was mid-October, 2009. Around 11:30, the cab – a minivan similar to the one I had in the shop – arrived at the end of our driveway nearest the house. As I walked out the front door, the driver reached across and pushed the passenger door open. I'd never had a cab door opened for me before, much less an invitation to get in the front seat – but then, I'd never had a cab ride in Fargo, either.

How Fargo of you, I thought.

"Where you headed?" The driver asked as I hopped in. He was about thirty, I guessed, with the look of an athlete who no longer had much time for sports.

"Toscana," I said. "It's a great little Italian restaurant down on Broadway."

"I've seen it," he said. "On the corner of Second Avenue, right?"

"Yeah. My van's in the shop, so I'm going to borrow my wife's car and run some errands today, and we decided to meet for lunch first."

"So how long have you lived in Reiles Acres?" he asked as we pulled out of the driveway.

"A little over four years now."

"How do you like it?" He was looking around at the beautiful one-acre lots on our street. We were just passing Chad's house, the neighbor who had rescued Charlene when she'd gotten stuck in our driveway our first winter here. Chad and his family have a beautiful two-story home.

"We love it," I said. "It's great for families. We moved here from Arizona so our kids would have a good place to grow up, and it's been *great*. What's your name?"

"Kevin. You're Marc, right?"

"Right." He must have known my name from the reservation I'd made with the cab company. We were approaching the end of our street and had to turn either north or south onto 45th Street. The shortest route would be to head south straight into town, but if we went that way we'd hit a mile and a half of bumpy dirt road on the way. Kevin hesitated, knowing, I suspected, that would be the least expensive route for me, but not the smoothest. "Why don't you just head north to County Road Twenty?" I suggested. "Then we can take that past the airport to University Drive."

"Okay," Kevin nodded and turned left. "Arizona, huh?" He was driving slowly over one of Reiles Acres' many speed bumps. "Why'd you come to Fargo? Weather too good for you down there?" We both laughed. Then Kevin asked the question almost everyone around here asks when they learn we're from Arizona: "Did you grow up here?"

If you live here, people around here assume you must be from here. Fargo is a secret, known only to those who've spent some time in this part of the upper Midwest. It's an "everybody knows" sort of a secret in this part of the world: *Of course no one understands Fargo who hasn't spent time in Fargo.* Just like "everyone knows" that North Dakota is no tourist Mecca. So if you're not from here, how could you possibly know you wanted to live here?

"Well," I said as we accelerated away from Reiles Acres' last stop sign, "My wife's best friend lives here, so we came to visit her about nine years ago, and fell in love with the place. I didn't know there was anywhere like this before then, you know, the way people treat one another, more concerned with relationships and each other than *stuff*. Any-way, we were getting worried in Arizona as our kids got close to their teenage years. We couldn't find a high school that didn't have a high drop out rate and drug problems and a lot of gang culture – that's sort of an oxymoron, I know, *gang culture...*" – Kevin started to laugh – "...but you know what I mean, a lot of pants below butts and other celebrations of dumbness..."

Kevin was laughing pretty hard now, like someone who had witnessed more "gang culture" than I imagined your typical Fargo cab driver might have seen. I was soon to learn otherwise. "But anyway," I continued, "in the first part of 2005, a bunch of stuff that had been holding us in Arizona just disappeared – my wife needed a change and left her job, the management at the kids' school changed and started going downhill, I finished a writing project – anyway, when all that stuff happened, we moved up here faster than you could say *freeze your butt off*."

Kevin laughed again. We were now on County Road 20, heading east toward the north end of Hector International Airport. As the road started to curve northward around the runways, I could see the Jet Center off to the right, servicing the surprising number of private jets flying in and out of Fargo on an almost hourly basis. About a month earlier, I'd met the very friendly lady, Dawndi, who manages the Center. We'd been in the produce section of a nearby grocery store. Don't ask me how we started talking or how I found out what she did. I don't remember, we were chatting about apples or something, it was the kind of conversation that happens all the time in Fargo. But noticing the Center as we drove by, I thought of her. Whenever I go somewhere in Fargo it's like that – the places along the way remind me of the people I've met.

Kevin had stopped laughing now. I decided to return the question he'd originally asked me: "So are you from around here, Kevin?"

"I grew up here, but we just moved back from San Diego earlier this year."

"San Diego, huh?" I figured I was probably about to hear a very interesting story, the kind of story I'd heard a few other times since moving here. "So why'd you go to San Diego, and what brought you back to Fargo?"

"Well," Kevin said. "My wife and I moved to San Diego for a job offer I got after I graduated from NDSU. I ended up as the assistant manager for the largest Ford Dealership in the San Diego area. But then we had a baby, and about a year ago, with the second one on the way," – we were now turning right off of County Road 20 onto University Drive, which would take us south through the heart of north Fargo – "we decided we'd had enough of San Diego. We knew if we didn't move back soon, we might get stuck. You know, you buy a little house there, it's a half-million dollar mortgage, and if real estate prices dip – like they do pretty often in California – you can't sell it. Both our parents live here, and they wanted us to move back, and it's still a few years before they retire, so we moved back about eight months ago."

So Kevin had been the assistant manager of the largest Ford dealership in San Diego less than a year ago, probably pulling down six figures, or close to it. Now he was giving me a cab ride from Reiles Acres to Moorhead, so his kids would be able to grow up in a sane – well, no, *remarkably sane* – place. *How Fargo of you*, I thought, looking over at him.

"Well, Kevin, I've heard other stories like yours since we moved here. I've even seen some demographic studies that say that's a pretty typical pattern around here, kid grows up on the farm, gets a good work ethic... or someplace like a farm – did you grow up on a farm?"

"No, my dad had a repair shop I helped in."

"Yeah, that kind of a thing. Anyway, kids get a good work ethic around here so they excel in school, but they don't want to stay on the farm or... or in the *repair shop...*" – Kevin chuckled a bit and nodded – "...so when they graduate from college with honors and get offered a good-paying job in some big city, off they go. But then, most are back in less than ten years. *Most*, according to a couple of studies I've heard about. And when they come back they usually take a job that pays maybe half of what they were making in the big city. Because they grew up here, and they're spoiled, you know, you get spoiled when you live here for a while – I know I am, and I didn't even grow up here, I've just lived here four years now. Anyway, it makes perfect sense to me, people don't want to raise their kids in other places when they know what's here."

Kevin was nodding. Then the light turned yellow ahead, and he began slowing. It was the first stoplight we'd come to, about four miles into our little journey, at the corner of University and 32nd Avenue North. I could see the Fargodome about a half-mile ahead, where Bon Jovi had just put on a sold-out concert a couple of nights earlier. The sights and sounds of the Elton John/Billy Joel concert I'd gone to with Anastasia a few weeks earlier began drifting through my head.

"I believe that," Kevin said, nodding. "We know three other couples from school who all did the same thing we did, and have moved back in the last couple of years, just like us. We all got together a few months ago and swapped stories. It was pretty funny. We were all laughing a lot."

"And I bet they're all making a lot less than they were."

"Pretty much."

"Like you."

"Pretty much."

"Well, *How Fargo of you.*"

"Huh?" Kevin looked at me quizzically.

"How Fargo of you. It's just an expression I use for all the things I never experienced before I came here. You know, how *Fargo* of you..."

Kevin started to chuckle and nod.

"Like when we first moved in," I continued to explain, "I hired a carpenter I barely knew to put a doggie door in, and he did a great job, but then he refused to let me pay him – insisted it was *a housewarming gift.* And I hardly knew the guy at that point, we'd just said 'hi' to each other at a concert. Or a few months ago when my son and I were having dinner in Hunter and a couple we didn't even know, you know, we'd never even met them, paid for our dinners and left the restaurant before we even knew they'd done it or who they were. We only found out they'd paid for us later when we went to pay and the waitress told us a couple who'd left had already paid for us."

The light turned green. We started moving again.

Kevin was smiling. "Didn't even know'em, huh?"

"I still haven't the faintest clue who they were," I said. "For a while after we moved here I had no idea what to say when this stuff would happen, or what to say about you and your friends giving up your high-paying jobs in the big city so your kids can grow up in a good place. Then one day it just sort of came out, I just found myself saying, '*Oh... How Fargo of you.*'"

Kevin started laughing again, pretty hard this time. I started getting a little concerned about staying on the road. But his gales soon subsided, and when he could speak again he said, "That's good. How **Fargo** of you. That's *really* good."

About eight weeks later, Kevin's story would give me the insight I needed to realize just how good it was.

*   *   *

I was in the conference room adjacent to Joan Deal's office, off the large, skylit atrium at the center of Media Production's beautiful offices. Joan was sitting across the corner of the conference table from me, looking at a few pages I'd emailed her and chuckling. "This is *great*," she said, shaking her head and smiling. "I *love* it!"

It was December 2009, about two months since my cab ride with Kevin. I'd first met Joan about ten months earlier, in a business meeting where I was acting as a consultant. I'd been extremely impressed with her calm, pleasant approach to solving problems. She was *very* Fargo. And sharp as a Bowie knife.

This time, it was Joan who was acting as the consultant. It had all started late last week, when I'd called my friend Adrienne Olson, the Director of Communications for the Fargo-Moorhead Chamber of Commerce.

"Hello, this is Adrienne." She has a great voice, businesslike but warm. *Fargo.*

"Hi, Adrienne, this is Marc de Celle." I suddenly got the image of Adrienne and her husband, who happen to live in Reiles Acres, walking by our house with their new baby about a week earlier, when I'd been out doing some yard work. We'd waved to one other, then I'd walked over and we'd chatted for a couple of minutes. They were a gorgeous family.

"Oh, *hi Marc.* How are you?"

"I'm doing pretty good, thanks. How's your baby and your husband?" I asked, unable to conceal my almost complete inability to remember the names of people I haven't spent much time with.

"They're great," she said with her warm voice sincerely intact, ignoring my failure to remember the names of the two people closest to her in all the world. "What can I do for you?"

"Well, Adrienne, I have a question. I'm thinking about putting on an event, but I have no idea what I'm doing. So I need to know who I should consult about how to put on a really successful event in Fargo. And since the Chamber does more big, successful events than anyone else around here, I figured you'd be the perfect person to ask."

"Well, we put on most of our events ourselves, but when I have a really big event, or a problem with an event I can't figure out, I go to Joan Deal..." – the name was ringing a bell in my head, but I couldn't quite place it – "...she's the person we go to when we need the best event expertise we can find."

"What was her name again?" I was scrambling to get a pen and paper.

"Joan Deal, at Media Productions." *Media Productions...* suddenly the image came to me, the nice offices, the face, the *demeanor.* The smarts!

"Oh!" I practically yelled. "Joan Deal! I *know* Joan Deal! I *love* Joan Deal! She's great. I had no idea she was an event expert!"

Adrienne was laughing a little. My enthusiasm is sometimes not so much contagious as *funny.* "Yep," Adrienne said through a chuckle, "that's who we use when we need the best event expertise. Joan."

"Great, Adrienne. Thanks *a lot.* I'll give her a call..."

About a minute later I was on the phone to Media Productions, learning that Joan was down in Minneapolis for a few days – putting on a big event for a client there. I got her email address and sent her a simple outline of my idea. Later that day I got this reply:

Marc,

Fabulous! What a *great* idea! I *love* it! Let's get together early next week after I get back in town.

Joan

Sitting across from Joan in the same conference room where we'd first met ten months earlier, a million thoughts were all trying to make their way through my head at once. I had no idea how to put on an event. All I really had was an idea. I was feeling very thankful to be sitting across from perhaps the best event expert in Fargo. I was even happier that she exuded calm serenity. I needed all the calm serenity I could get.

"I hope you don't mind, Marc," Joan was now saying, "but as I mentioned when we set up our appointment, I shared this with Lee Massey, our president. He just *loves* it. He might drop by while you're here."

"No, that's fine. As long as he knows I don't want word getting out about it just yet."

"I told him. So, how did you come up with this?"

"Well, first, Joan, let me tell you – as I think I made clear in the notes I sent you – I don't have any money to spend." When Joan had told me the president of Media Productions might drop in on us, I wanted to make sure he didn't have the wrong idea. "So if we do an event, it's got to pay for itself, it's got to pay for you and me and the caterers or anyone else who helps put it on." Joan was nodding, with sort of a Mona Lisa smile. "I mean, if we'd have been having this conversation a few years ago, when we first moved up here, I'd've had some money to spend. But, uh, you know, the last year hasn't been the best economically speaking, and it's been pretty tight since we moved here anyway, so I just want you to understand, I don't want to lead you on or anything."

"I understand," Joan said. "You alluded to that in your emails."

"Okay. Just so you know."

"So tell me the story," Joan said, eyes warm. She showed not the least concern about my inability to pay her or her company anything. "How'd you come to this idea?"

"Well, I was in Minneapolis on business last month – and you know, I think half the frustration level people experience in big cities is from the driving…"

"Oh, I *know*," Joan nodded, rolling her eyes, as though the memories of her recent visit were still mildly irritating.

"I mean, every exit is different and, you know, it's just so frantic…"

"Tell me about it."

"And Minneapolis is nothing compared to LA, where I used to live. But after being up here for a while... We're spoiled here, aren't we?"

"Aren't we?" Joan chuckled, nodding some more.

"Anyway, I was down there for a few days on business, and I don't like being away from my kids and my wife for that long, so after I got back I was thinking about it, and I decided I needed to come up with a way to introduce myself to the Fargo business community in a major way. Other-wise, my business is likely to grow more out of town than in town. I mean, I'd much rather work twice as many hours for half as much per hour, and be able to spend evenings at home with my family, and get to know Fargo better, too."

"Yeah, that makes sense." Joan was nodding me on.

"And an event seemed a logical way to introduce myself."

"Mmm-hmm?" Joan's eyebrows were raised now, expectantly. I still hadn't answered her question.

"So I sat down and made a list of questions about what I would want out of such an event, visual questions about what I'd want it to look like, starting with the result I'd want after it was all over."

"I always start from the end," Joan said with a smile and another nod.

"Well, that's good. It's always nice to hear Fargo's leading event expert tell me I've done what she'd do." That got a laugh. "So anyway, I asked myself how I wanted people who came to the event to feel after the event was all over and they were leaving, or maybe even a couple of days or a few weeks after the event..."

"Mmm-hmm..."

"And basically, I just wanted them to feel happy and uplifted, you know, have a really warm feeling about it..."

"Mmm-hmm..."

"So after I answered that question I mentally jumped to the front of the event, and asked myself what would make people in Fargo want to come to an event."

"Yeah..." She was nodding a bit more emphatically. I could tell she was starting to see what I'd seen.

"And immediately, when I asked myself that question, I thought of putting on a *How Fargo of You* event. I mean, it's just a phrase I've been using the last few years that everyone around here gets a kick out of, because they all know what I'm talking about, they all have stories like the ones in those notes I emailed you. At first, I was thinking I'd just use *How Fargo of You* as part of the event, sort of a come-on, but the more I thought about it, the more I realized I should just put on a *How Fargo of You* event. For one thing, it's a lot more fun talking about Fargo than explaining what I do. For another, *How Fargo of You* is actually a pretty good example of what I do, discovering the most important but neglected aspect of something and finding a way to communicate it."

"Well, it's *really* great," Joan said. "As I read these notes I got really warm feelings," she said, holding her hands over her heart. "It makes me feel proud. I *love* it."

"Well, that's what I've been told by the half-dozen or so people I've run the idea by this last week. But I have no idea how to put on an event, Joan. And I'm not sure that timeline I outlined and sent you is even plausible. I can write the stories, and I can collect and edit other people's stories, because once I tell anyone around here a *How Fargo of You* story, it reminds them of similar things that have happened to them..."

Joan was nodding. "So you think a book should be part of it?" she asked. "I remember you mentioned something about the possibility of a book in here..." She was looking through her print-outs of my emails.

"Well, maybe, but I've had some misgivings about it..."

Joan suddenly looked out through the glass conference room walls toward the front door. "Oh, there's Lee," she said. "Remember I passed your stuff on to our president?"

"Yeah," I said, turning my head toward where Joan was looking. I couldn't see anyone from where I was sitting.

"Well, he's here now." Joan was rising from her chair. "I know he wants to meet you." She was heading toward the conference room door. I followed.

"Oh, and he's got Roger with him. Roger Reierson is the CEO of Flint Communications, our parent company."

I knew about Flint Communications. Based in Fargo, Flint is the largest advertising/marketing/PR firm between Minneapolis and Denver. I knew they'd been in business for over sixty years – longer than about 99 percent of the advertising agencies in the world. And now, their CEO was just down the hall.

*   *   *

We were waiting for the stoplight at University and 19th Avenue to turn green. The Fargodome now loomed across the street. I looked out the passenger side window of the minivan cab. In the distance down 19th Avenue I could see the sleek curves and jaunty corners of the Incubator, the hippest looking building this side of Minneapolis. I smiled a little, remembering the award-winning architect who had designed it, Kim Kelsey, who I'd gotten to know when I'd done a project for the firm she worked for, R.L. Engebretson, a couple of years earlier. One day, my daughter Anastasia, who was then twelve, had been with me when I'd dropped in to pick something up, and Kim, who is exceptionally friendly and kind, had introduced herself. Then Kim – who looked every bit of the eight months pregnant she was at the time – had shown Anastasia around her office and talked with her about designing buildings for a few minutes. Anastasia had been so impressed by the experience she began thinking about architecture as a profession.

The light turned green. We crossed over 19th Avenue and passed the Fargodome. We were now entering the part of North Fargo dominated by North Dakota State University.

"Well, Kevin, even our story's kind of the same," I said. "I mean, my wife's got a resume most companies cry over, only two major employers over thirty years, one a Fortune fifty company, constant promotions and increasing responsibilities wherever they put her, the whole bit. She's never had a problem getting a good job in her life. But after we moved here, she worked as a temp for Microsoft for the first three years making less than half of what she was in Arizona, really, the kind of pay she was getting in her early twenties, when the dollar was worth a lot more – so she was really making less than she has in at least a quarter-century, despite the fact that she's built a helluva resume throughout her life. And it seems like this is true of a lot of people around here. We have one of the lowest unemployment rates in the country, yeah, but we also have experienced executives driving cabs."

"Tell me about it," Kevin chuckled, nodding.

"For example, my wife's best friend at Microsoft has a master's degree in human resources, and she worked there as a temp for over a year before getting a good permanent clerical job there, which she is really happy to have. Because this area's just loaded with overqualified, underemployed people like her. And you. And my wife. And me. And your friends. We're just loaded with people who are sacrificing a lot of income because they want to raise their families in this culture. Really, if you think about it, Fargo's sort of a two-edged sword that way. I mean, on one side, we have this great culture we're part of. But on the other side, there's so many people giving up so much income to be here, the pool of talent we all compete with in this job market is just *extraordinary*."

"Sort of heaven for employers," Kevin said.

"Although I'm not sure any big companies besides Microsoft have really figured that out yet," I replied. "I mean, why should they hire permanent positions when they can get people the caliber of my wife as *temps?*"

"Well," Kevin said, "maybe that explains why Microsoft just built that big new building over there and they're still expanding here, even during the recession."

"I think they have to be pretty happy with the bang they get for their Fargo buck," I agreed. "Even though they could probably put a lot of these new operations in India, where the labor rates are maybe a quarter of what they are here."

There was momentary silence, then Kevin spoke, slowly and thoughtfully. "I know what you're talking about, the double-edged sword. If we didn't already have a lot of family here, we couldn't afford to move here. The only reason we were able to move back was because we have a really good support system, with both our families here and our parents still working."

"Hey, the only reason we're able to be here is we had a decent little nest egg when we came."

It was silent for a moment. We were passing the central part of NDSU. I thought of my friend Greg Cook, Chair of the Chemistry Department, probably in his office right now, about a quarter mile from our cab, who'd probably devoted a couple dozen hours to helping me edit several science-related articles I'd written over the last couple of years, never asking for anything in return but instead, inviting me to several of the renowned wine-tasting parties – replete with some of his gourmet cooking – he and his wife put on in their home. "You know, Kevin, it's not that there isn't a lot of money here, we've got private corporate jets zooming in and out sometimes three or four times an hour, believe me I know, when the wind is blowing east-west our house is right below the flight path. And I've met a bunch of people here who I'm sure make six figures. But when you look on the *Ladders* – you know, that website advertising only six-figure jobs – I have yet to see *a single posting* from Fargo. Not that I need six figures, I'd be really happy with half that right now. But I've been looking at the *Ladders* for over a year, and almost every day they've got a job or two listed in the Twin cities I could apply for. But I have yet to see *one single posting* for a job here in over a year of looking. It's not that we're that much smaller, we've got about two hundred thousand people in the Fargo metro area now, so that's about one-tenth the size of the Twin Cities, so in theory we'd have one-tenth the listings. But *nada.* I've come to the conclusion that very few people with high-paying jobs in Fargo get them through a normal interview process. Because everyone who's in a position to be hiring anyone for a six-figure job already knows a dozen people in town who could do the job. Fargo's basically a giant personnel pool of overqualified, underemployed people like you, and a lot of these people have known each other for decades, so they know each other's character, which is something you can't really uncover in a normal interview process, and here especially, character's probably more important than anything else. I mean, why would anyone hire somebody for an important job through a normal anonymous hiring process when they already know several people who could do that job really well, people they've known for decades, so they know what they're *really* like? So this economy is very unlike any I've ever seen before, sort of an economy of... well, an economy of tremendous generosity on one side, but then Adam Smith's 'invisible hand' comes in on the other side to balance it out, and makes it pretty tight – tough, even, sometimes."

"I *hear* you, Marc, it's a two-edged sword. That's why I spent a lot of time just hanging around and helping out at a few dealerships for a while after we came back, until one of them started actually paying me to do a few things. There's no way I'm just going to snag a good job out of the blue around here like I might in San Diego."

"So you're doing a little work for one of the dealerships in town now, along with driving cab?"

"Yeah, nothing very important, just a few hours a week and on weekends doing odd jobs, but it keeps my hand in and let's people in the industry know I'm here, gets my name and what I've done out there at least."

It was quiet again. Kevin turned left off of University onto 6th Avenue.

*   *   *

Joan and I were back in the conference room. When Joan introduced me to Lee Massey, the president of Media Productions, he'd been almost effusive about the few pages of notes I'd emailed Joan. Lee had the enthusiastic countenance of a twenty year old, though I was pretty sure he was a young looking forty-something. I'd felt compelled to tell him right away I didn't have any money to spend – I just wanted to make sure I wasn't leading him on, that he wasn't under the misimpression that I was ready to lay out a bunch of money to put on an event. It was the kind of thing I'd tended to do since developing my own ideas about how business ought to be done some years ago, which had often rubbed people the wrong way in other places – places where façade and secrecy often trumped openness and transparency – but my direct approach seemed to fit right in here in Fargo, and my frankness didn't seem to dampen Lee's enthusiasm in the least. He'd simply gone on to introduce me to Roger Reierson, the CEO of Flint Communications, who'd been chatting with Joan about something while Lee and I talked. Roger is a tall, slender, athletic-looking man in his fifties, I'd guess.

"Very nice to meet you," I said as we shook hands.

"Glad to meet you."

"Marc's got a really exciting idea," Lee chimed in, "that he's talking about with Joan."

"I'm just here to get Joan's advice about an event I'm thinking about," I told Roger, "because my excellent research skills ferreted out the fact that she's pretty much Fargo's leading event expert."

"That she is," Roger nodded with a chuckle, then glanced warmly at Joan. "Well, let's not interrupt you any further. C'mon, Lee."

"Nice meeting you, Marc," Lee waved with an exuberant smile as he and Roger headed out the other side of the sunlit atrium.

"Very nice meeting you, too, Lee." I waved back.

Joan and I were now back in the conference room. "So, Marc, where were we?" Joan asked. "I think we were talking about the possibility of a book to go with this."

"Well, yeah, Joan, here's the thing. From the first time I heard the words *How Fargo of You* falling from my lips, I knew it would make the perfect title for a book full of these stories. But I've always had a lot of misgivings about it, too, and that's why I've never pursued it."

"Misgivings?" Joan asked.

"Yeah, I don't want to wreck Fargo. And I think these stories have the power to do that. I don't mean my personal *How Fargo of You* stories, I'm talking about the thousands of untold *How Fargo of You* stories within a ten mile radius of where we're sitting right now. Look Joan, I just moved from Phoenix, which was a pretty good place to grow up forty years ago, and now it's a mess. And a lot of the reason, probably the only significant reason it's a mess is *too many people coming in too fast*. When I was a kid, the Phoenix area had a population of about a half-million, and now it has seven times that, three-and-a-half million, and I don't think any culture, no matter how strong, can assimilate that kind of influx without being destroyed in the process, because, I mean, if you have a culture that's *this* big" – I made a little grapefruit-sized ball shape with my hands – "and then you take *this* many people" – I now spread my arms wide, like I was holding a large, imaginary beach ball – "from outside that culture and try to push them all in" – I now shoved the imaginary beach ball in on the spot where I'd first made a grapefruit-sized shape with my hands – "there's just going to be nothing left of that original culture when it's over."

"Mmm-hmm…"

"And I worry that telling these stories to people outside of this area has the power to do that, because if you think about it for a minute, this sets itself up for a *Chicken Soup for the Soul* kind of a thing, where different people tell their stories in the same book or books…"

"Mmm-hmm…"

"I mean, it probably seems like I'm getting ahead of myself, but I don't think I am. There's probably at least a hundred million people in the U.S. who are like me, or like I was, and have no idea that a culture like this actually exists right here, right now, and they would be very hungry for it if they knew it was here, and some would flock, just like my family did. So the potential success of such a book scares the hell out of me, and I don't want to do something if I have misgivings about it being successful. It's sort of a terrible paradox, the thing that would make such a book successful and even important, perhaps, would be letting people know that this kind of a culture is possible and does actually exist in a fairly high-tech little metropolis in the 21st Century, but that's the same thing that could make the book just awful for Fargo if it took off, because until now this culture's been largely a secret, and a collection of these stories could start to change that pretty fast. I mean there's probably only a few million people who know what it's like here right now. The U.S. population is a hundred times that, so letting the cat out of the bag in any significant way could ultimately be very destructive. I think the reason Fargo has grown a lot over the last few decades and managed to keep its culture intact is because almost everyone who's moved here is from around here" – I thought of Kevin and our cab ride as I said this – "I mean from local farming communities and the general region, so Fargo hasn't had to assimilate a lot of outsiders, really. I don't mean outsiders like my family can't become part of this culture, but it takes time, and too many of us coming too fast – well, remember that video of the floodwaters washing away the pedestrian bridge in the park last year?"

I shut up for a second, and there was silence. No "Mmm-hmms" from Joan. Not even a nod. She looked thoughtful, reflective. It was too much silence.

"Because all I've done at this point, Joan" I continued, "is made a few pages of notes and shown them to a half-dozen people, two of whom have never been here, and so far everyone who's seen it has said something about a book and that they'd want to buy a half-dozen copies to send to people they know…"

Suddenly, the image of my cab ride with Kevin came flooding back to me full-force. "Oh…" I heard myself say, off in the distance somewhere. It was an obvious revelation, the best kind. Until now, I'd only been telling stories from one side of the "doubled-edged sword" Kevin and I had discussed. Kevin's story – and the thousands like it, like my own family's – were every bit as much *How Fargo of You* stories as any others, perhaps even more so. The tough, unrelenting, underlying realities of the Fargo culture were what made the fairytale side of Fargo possible. Without the extreme self-reliance of people like Kevin – and our neighbor Chad, and the people of Hunter, and the hundreds of others I'd met – the generosity of Fargo simply would not be possible, just as, that bright, November morning when the kids and I had explored the wonders following our first winter storm, we would have frozen to death without the layers of high-tech insulation on our bodies that made our comfort and mobility possible.

"What are you thinking about, Marc?" I heard a voice in the distance.

I suddenly realized where I was. I realized there had been silence. Joan's voice was bringing me back. Her calm face, then the conference table, then the offices around us materialized once again. I had a new kind of *How Fargo of You* story to tell her.

*   *   *

Turning off of University onto 4th Avenue, we were now just a few minutes away from Toscana. "So, Kevin, you got any good *How Fargo of You* stories?" I asked, still two months away from realizing he'd already told me one of the most important *How Fargo of You* stories I would ever hear.

"Hmmm..." He peered ahead as if his memories were mixing with the traffic. "Well, a few. One that comes to mind wasn't in Fargo, though, it was about fifty miles east of here, in the lakes country in Minnesota."

"Oh, yeah," I nodded, "I just use *Fargo* because it's sort of in the middle of where all this stuff happens, and it has a really nice ring to it, you know, *How **Fargo** of You*. But there's a lot of stories like this anywhere within a few hundred miles of here – I've even heard a couple of great *How Fargo of You* stories from Nebraska, you know, so... so anyway, what happened in the lakes country?"

"Well, I was still in college, and one summer some buddies and I were out there doing some fishing. We were in an old beater, you know, a college car – I think it was John's car, one of the guys – old tires and everything, and on the way from one lake to another we got a flat. In the middle of nowhere. We could see a farmhouse a ways off, but that was about it, we were on one of those roads where another car might come by every twenty minutes, you know, if you're lucky. And we started trying to jack it up with this really lousy jack. Then an old farmer drives up. He was from the farmhouse. Seen us from the barn or something. And he gets out of his truck and sort of looks sideways at what we're doing and says, 'Hmmm… looks like you boys could use a *jack.*' And we all started laughing."

Kevin was now turning right onto Broadway. We were about a minute from the restaurant.

"So anyway, the farmer told us to hold on, and he drove back to his barn, and a few minutes later he brings back a tractor jack. I mean, it was almost half as big as the car. And we all started laughing some more. And we got it out and it lifted the car like a Tonka toy. So in no time we were done, and as we were lowering the car back down, the farmer's wife shows up in her little car and brings out a big plate of sandwiches."

"Are you kidding?" I asked, laughing.

"'I bet you boys are *hungry,*' she says. So we all had sandwiches right there on the road with the farmer and his wife, and he told us to go about ten miles straight down the road until we got to the next little town, and he told us who to see to get the spare patched, you know, 'Ah'm not kiddin', you git that spare patched 'fore you do any more fishin' 'cause you'll prob'ly need it again 'fore you git back t' Fargo 'cause 'those tars're balder than a nekked jay-bird.'"

Kevin and I both laughed at his impression of the down-to-earth, generous, competent farmer. "So we did just what he told us to, and we told the guy who patched the tire the whole story, and since we filled up on gas there he didn't charge us to patch the tire."

"*Nothing?*" I said, laughing some more.

Kevin shook his head and shrugged. "Hey, those Minnesotans can be just about as *Fargo* as anybody." We laughed some more.

"That's a great story," I said, still soaking in the image of the roadside picnic with the farmer and his wife and the four college guys out fishing. I never get tired of hearing these stories. They always make me feel *really* good – and so happy, all over again, that we found this place.

"Yeah, it was. It was pretty *Fargo*," Kevin said, and we both laughed again. We were stopping. Looking around, I realized Kevin had just pulled the cab up to the front door of Toscana.

"Hey, it was great meeting you, Kevin," I said, having no idea, yet, just how great it was. I paid the fare and added a five. "I really enjoyed it. Good luck to you and your family."

"Hey, thanks, Marc. I enjoyed it, too. Thanks a lot."

*   *   *

I was finishing the story about my cab ride with Kevin eight weeks earlier. Joan was nodding and smiling again.

"Mmm-hmm..."

"So, I guess that means a book *should* be part of it. As long as I tell Kevin's story and others like it, like my own family's, people should get a realistic enough of a picture. If people understand the sacrifices they're making by moving here, I think the only people who'd be seriously tempted to come would be people most likely to be okay, people who'd tend to fit into the local culture pretty easily. I mean, people who are willing to forgo a lot of stuff in exchange for a real sense of community, or entrepreneurial types with great ideas for new businesses who want to take advantage of the high work ethic."

"I think you may be right, Marc." Joan was nodding thoughtfully. She seemed to be rolling my ideas around in her head, and deciding they were okay.

"So, I guess the big question is this, Joan. What do you think about that timeline I sent you? Is it plausible?" One of the emails I'd sent Joan before our meeting was a proposed timeline for putting together a *How Fargo of You* event.

"Well, we can do it right or we can do it rushed. And it seems a bit rushed," she said, simply stating the facts.

"So what do you think I should do?" I asked. I still had a million thoughts all trying to make their way through my head at once.

"Hmm... I think..." she was looking at the papers she'd printed out from my emails. Then she looked up at me and smiled. "I think you should write the book first."

The muscles in my neck, which I hadn't realized were tense, suddenly relaxed. The millions of thoughts clamoring for my attention were all floating away from me now, far, far away. I began to feel the way Joan looked: calm and serene. It was a moment, and I knew it. She was right and I knew it. And I knew, with a clarity and a simplicity I'd been longing for, exactly what I was going to do.

*   *   *

It's early April as I finish this chapter, the book is nearing completion, and I just met with Joan again last week. Again we talked about Kevin, and how his cab ride changed the direction of my life. And again I tried to discuss ways I might be able to pay for the help Joan has already given me. And again nothing came of it.

And again, there's only one possible thing to say.

How Fargo of You.

CHAPTER 10

Sandbags to Heaven

Are we there yet?

2010

Monday, March 15

"It was the youth that saved Fargo-Moorhead last year." Tom already had my attention, but now I was riveted. I knew I would soon need to start writing the biggest *How Fargo of You* story of them all – the story of the 2009 flood fight and perhaps,

though I hoped not, the story of the 2010 flood fight to come –
and I needed to find a way in. Something told me Tom had it.

"You mean college kids?" I asked.

"Not just college, high school kids, even junior high," he
replied.

Tom had just finished sharpening my daughter's ice skates.
Serious skaters – both hockey players and figure skaters, like my
daughter – come from hundreds of miles around to get their
skates sharpened by Tom. Some mail them in from places as far
away as California. There just aren't many people who can do it
right. Tom does it right.

"The first time I saw it," he continued, "was in Rose Creek
last year. We had to get the sandbags up to a certain height by
the end of the day to stay ahead of the river, or the water would
just start pouring over. If that happened, it could pretty much be
over for the whole city, like it was in New Orleans after the first
break in the levees. I looked at how far we had to go," Tom
shook his head as he remembered, "and I said, 'Man, that's a *lot*
of work.' We were working as hard as we could but falling
further behind. The river was rising faster than the sandbags.
Then the kids starting coming in on buses. And the sandbags
just went up" – Tom's right hand was now karate-chopping the
air sideways, each chop higher than the last – "level after level
after level. I got a really good idea of how they built the
pyramids. It's amazing what manual labor can accomplish
when young people are involved and organized."

Tom is a big man with a powerful build, well over six feet, somewhere in his forties. He moves easily, almost gently – a habit I suspect he acquired at some point in his life so as not to frighten the rest of us. He has the look of a Viking who has taken up shaving, a look common to a lot of men of Scandinavian ancestry in this part of the country. As soon as you see one of these men, it's immediately clear why Europe was sort of a buffet for these people. Which is just to say I wasn't listening to some milktoasty old fart prattling on about the wonderful energy of youth. Tom could clearly move some sandbags in his own right, which was how we'd gotten on the subject in the first place. As soon as he was done with work at one o'clock, he would be heading south to join the new, rapidly escalating sandbagging efforts of 2010.

Ten days ago, the snow drift in the front of our house had been about seven feet high – a good foot higher than we'd ever seen it before. There had been a lot of snowfall over the winter, not just in Fargo, but across all sixty-five thousand square miles of the Red River Basin. When it all melted, it would flow into the Red River, eventually coming right through the middle of Fargo-Moorhead on its way northward to Lake Winnipeg in Canada. So I'd really been hoping for a nice, slow, gradual spring warm-up, with no rain. The slower the melt, the more time the Red would have to move all that water past us toward Canada, and the lower the crest of the river would be.

No such luck. We'd just had ten warm, rainy days. The snowdrift in front of our house was down to about two feet, an icy little remnant of its former glory. And the sandbagging had begun. Again. The Red was expected to rise from its current 12-foot level to over 30 feet in less than a week.

"I heard a geology professor from NDSU on Prairie Public radio the other day," I said to Tom. "He was saying he's seen about a dozen hundred-year floods here in the last three decades. If the Red River Valley had weather like this a hundred years ago, nobody would have built a town here. If they had, it just would have been washed away every few years."

"That's right," Tom nodded. He rang up the bill for my daughter's skates on the cash register. "We're going to have to start to erect more permanent dikes."

It was ten a.m. There were only a couple of other customers in the store where Tom works – the *Outdoorsman* – and they were being taken care of by other staff. I was glad. I wanted to hear more.

"But Tom," I said, "There are such tremendous problems with getting anywhere near enough money for the kind of diversion project we need."

"The problem," Tom said, "is we did too good of a job. We did too good of a job in ninety-seven, and we did too good of a job last year. You know, last year, there were a lot of people from FEMA in town during the flood who liked to hang out here..." – Tom's hand swept the room – the *Outdoorsman* has everything you'd imagine a store with that name might hold, from fishing poles to guns, camping supplies to archery equipment – "... and a lot of them have done emergency work around the country for decades. And they just couldn't get over how different it is here…"

"They probably couldn't get in edgewise," I guessed, "because everything that needed to be done was already being done by a bunch of volunteers."

"Exactly."

*   *   *

A Year Earlier

2009

Thursday, March 19

We have about a week.

Less than a month ago, the National Weather Service predicted the Red River would crest sometime around mid-April, with a 60 percent chance of rising above 35 feet. I hadn't been too concerned. In 2006, during our first April here, the Red had crested at just over 37 feet. That was the year of our first magical Fargo winter storm, the one we'd enjoyed so much at the end of November, a little over three months after we moved in. Then there'd been the snows in January of that year, which had led to Charlene getting stuck in our driveway, from which our neighbor Chad had rescued her. Anyway, all that snow and ice had started melting in late March, and there had been quite a bit of activity along the Red River, diking and sandbagging – but no serious talk of impending disaster that I recall. I remember watching the fields just to the west of our house slowly fill with water, a couple of feet shy of coming up onto the streets of Reiles Acres. It was a little disconcerting at first, but once it was clear the water would come no further, I'd actually enjoyed it. For several days the sunsets had reminded me of living on the Gulf Coast of Florida years ago, where I'd loved to watch the reds, oranges and yellows reflecting across the glassy-smooth waters of the Gulf of Mexico.

That was three years ago. Three weeks ago, I heard a report on Minnesota Public Radio that placed the odds of meeting or exceeding those 2006 river levels at just 25 percent – so there was close to a three out of four chance I'd get to enjoy those sunsets again, worry-free. Pretty good odds, I thought at the time. Winter snowfall was only a little above normal, the MPR reporter had explained, but heavy rains in the fall, followed by a quick freeze at the onset of winter, had trapped a lot of moisture in the Red River Valley. The Red River would be high this spring. But it didn't sound very dire.

Then, about a week ago, a snowstorm dumped ten more inches of snow, causing the National Weather Service to revise their earlier forecast slightly upwards – but only slightly.

Then today happened. The predictions changed *Big Time*. WDAY news anchor Dana Mogck is telling us the National

Weather Service has just released a new forecast, saying the Red could crest *before April, and might even surpass the modern high of just over 39 feet set in 1997.*

Now Kerstin Kealy, co-anchor of the WDAY ten o'clock newscast, is saying this is unlike anything Fargo has ever seen before. In 1997, when the highest crest in a hundred years – just over 39 feet – had been reached, there had been months to prepare, because record winter snowfall had made the coming flood obvious and inevitable. But this time, the extreme, immediate flood danger has caught everyone by surprise. Officials had all known Fargo would need to do some diking and sandbagging in April. Maybe even a lot of diking and sandbagging. But now, we're suddenly faced with the prospect of a record crest coming in about a week, well before April even arrives. The city will have to scramble to save itself, and the outcome is uncertain. *Very* uncertain.

As I watch the news, sitting on the bed with Charlene, images of New Orleans under water begin swirling in my head. They soon mix with scenes from Grand Forks, just sixty miles north of Fargo, scenes I'd watched on television from the safety of my Arizona living room twelve years before, during the record flood of 1997: Eerie scenes of a submerged downtown shot from helicopters, showing high rises simultaneously on fire and under water nearly to the second story – water that had come from a wildly overflowing Red River. I vaguely remember learning that the preparations for that flood fight were based on a crest forecast by the National Weather Service that turned out to be a few feet low – and that once water comes just a fraction of an inch over the sandbags, disaster is certain. I remember a conversation I had with Monty, an Arizona acquaintance whose parents lived in Grand Forks at the time. They and 50,000 other people had been evacuated, and once the waters receded, many of them had nothing to go back to except yucky, muddy, completely trashed homes that simply had to be cleared away before they could start again from scratch.

Meteorologist John Wheeler is now explaining that the sudden, unexpected warming spell of last week is largely to blame for the dramatically accelerated forecast. The Red River Basin – more than sixty-five thousand square miles of land that drains into the Red River – had a lot of snow and ice stored up from fall and winter. *Had.* The sudden warming spell of the last week has already melted most of that snow and ice, he explains, and all that water is now quickly heading into the Red River, straight toward us. But that, Wheeler adds, may only be part of the story. The latest weather forecast is foreboding: Our sudden warming trend may strengthen – and a major weather system is heading our way, due to arrive in several days.

Charlene and I are sitting on the bed, watching the news. There's a commercial break. At first, we don't move. Then we look at each other. "We'd better get all the irreplaceables up from the basement," Charlene says, first-things-first. "I don't care that much about the furniture. But the photographs and videos, our wedding stuff, stuff like that." I know exactly what she means. When she was about eight years old, her family lost their home in a fire. She'd told me that afterwards, they hadn't really missed the expensive stuff. It had been the personal, family remembrances, the simple things like photo albums and wedding dresses, yearbooks and letters, an old family Bible with the names of several previous generations inscribed inside – it was the loss of those kinds of things, irreplaceable things, that had really stung.

"Okay, I'll start bringing that stuff up in the next couple of days," I tell her, "as soon as I drain Lake de Celle."

I'm referring to the quarter-acre of water in our back yard. During the rapid warming spell of the last week, our entire neighborhood has turned from a beautiful blanket of white snow into a wet grassy mat with lots of little lakes, and the one we've dubbed "Lake de Celle," in our back yard, is probably the largest. The urgency is this: At the center of the lake is a large stand of trees which have been sitting in more than a foot of water for the last week.

We don't want to lose those beautiful trees. So I need to drain our lake. Yesterday. Especially if we're likely to see overland flooding submerging them again within a week.

Fortunately, Reiles Acres' mayor, Jefferson Bey – another clean-shaven Viking, 6'6", muscular, of understated mannerism and speech (like Tom, I suspect his manner is a kindness he adopted at some point in his life, as he grew larger, so as not to scare the rest of us) – anyway, Jefferson is a lot more efficient than I am, and has already had the snow removed from our drainage ditches using large digging equipment. So all I have to do is dig a little channel through the remaining ice and snow that separates Lake de Celle from the deep ditch at the front of our yard – a distance of about two hundred feet – and Lake de Celle will simply flow away.

Yeah, it's a far cry from the desert landscaping I grew up with. An hour or two per year spraying herbicide doesn't cut it around here. But I won't trade it back.

In North Dakota, you can't ignore nature, or take it for granted, or walk through life with the severe misimpression that we've somehow subdued it with air conditioning. Nature is clearly in charge. I'm not just talking yard work. That's the least of it. From black ice on the roads, which will spin your car around faster than you can say "oops," to snowdrifts on the side of those roads that can swallow and hide a vehicle and its occupants from searchers until spring, to a thousand other things big and small – lakes in yards to regional floods – nature constantly reminds you it's in charge, impartial and deadly if you're dumb or lazy. The best you can do is pay attention, stay calm, think ahead, be as prepared for any eventuality as possible and work hard to avoid catastrophe. On a regular basis.

Living here has convinced me that climate and character, in a free society, are inextricably linked. To be arrogant, aloof or careless around here, you'd have to be dumber than a skydiver in a snowstorm – and if you're that dumb around here, you're not around here long. You'll leave one way or another – train, plane or hearse.

Friday, March 20

I turn on the TV to the local news and start fixing lunch. I've been outside in the wet, mucky, icy, snowy yuck for a couple of hours, cutting a channel. Lake de Celle is now draining. My muddy snow boots are out in the garage.

I listen to the local broadcast coming from the other end of the living room as I start fixing some soup. The Red has just risen above the official flood stage of 18 feet. That's expected to more than double to over 36 feet *in less than a week.* Citing this unprecedented rise, the mayor has put out an unprecedented call for volunteers to fill and place *more than 2 million sandbags in the next five days.*

That's 400 thousand sandbags a day filled, transported and properly put in place.

In any other place I've ever lived, I wouldn't take his call seriously. I'd put it down to wishful thinking or political grandstanding or...

But I wonder. Fargo is unlike anyplace I've ever lived before. How different? Well, I guess I'm about to find out. I know Fargo's different. And I know it's for real. But this is a severe – perhaps insurmountable – test of the mettle of my adopted community.

It's a challenge from nature.

How deep does Fargo go?

Saturday, March 21

It's about three in the afternoon when I stop in front of the TV for a minute to catch my breath. It's about the fifth break I've taken today, not including lunch. Hauling boxes up from the basement isn't my favorite workout routine.

Each break I've taken, there's always been at least one local channel pre-empting regular programming to cover the flood preparations. They're showing scenes of bulldozers and dump trucks and caterpillars creating earthen levees all over town – but the reporters make it clear that most of the Red River's banks will have to be sandbagged along the length of their winding course through Fargo-Moorhead: Earthen levees and dikes can only be put up in a few areas where the huge machines used to make them can operate freely.

We're going to have to do most of this by hand.

Sunday, March 22

The storm is coming.

I'm watching John Wheeler again. The storm system he first warned about on Thursday is almost here – and it looks *wet*. *Very wet.*

Rain is the last thing we need. Flashing across the screen are live scenes from Wahpeton, 60 miles south of us, first victim

162

of the water heading north toward Fargo. There, streets and basements are already underwater. And on top of that, the entire region is about to get rain. Maybe a *lot* of rain.

Two million sandbags may not be enough, I think to myself.

Then Kirsten tells us more cheery news: The National Weather Service has announced the Red may crest in Fargo *before* the end of the week, *a day earlier than previously thought.*

I flip through the local stations several times over the next few hours as I finish bringing stuff up from the basement. The basement is pretty empty now, and it shows: Boxes are stacked all over the place up here – the dining room, living room and guest bedroom are all messy mazes of precariously stacked boxes. I survey the scene. It's almost like something you'd see on that new show *Hoarders,* about people who compulsively collect stuff all the time but can't bring themselves to ever give or throw anything away, so they can't hardly walk through their own homes. *I had no idea we had so much stuff down there.*

I flip through the channels some more. All the local stations are now all flood, all the time. There's an urgent call for volunteer sandbaggers. If you show up at the Fargodome or any of a dozen other makeshift emergency locations around town, you'll be told where volunteers are needed most, or transported there by bus. The news people all keep repeating this to the point where I actually consider heading over to the Fargodome myself – for about a second. *Who am I kidding?* I ask myself. *I'm not sure I'd be that much help on a good day. And right now, I'm pretty spent from the boxes-up-the-stairs routine.*

All the schools have cancelled classes for the coming week, so students – who came out in droves yesterday, on Saturday – can continue to help. Some businesses have closed indefinitely so their employees can help with the sandbagging effort, and many are arranging to continue their payroll through the week, at least in part. More than two hundred National Guard soldiers and airmen have now joined the volunteers at the Fargodome.

But two million sandbags may not be enough.

Monday, March 23

It's raining, raining, raining. Last night it started. Now it's raining some more. And it's supposed to keep raining until it gets colder by late Tuesday or early Wednesday, when it will snow instead.

Earlier today, while running an errand near the Fargodome that couldn't be put off – citizens have been asked to minimize travel to leave the streets as open as possible for vehicles and equipment engaged in the flood effort – I saw several 18-wheeler flatbed trucks transporting sandbags. Now, on the television screen, I'm looking at a live shot of the emergency sandbag-production facility inside the Fargodome, staffed by nearly a thousand volunteers. It's been dubbed "Sandbag Central." At least as big as a football field, it's a mix of people, piles of sand, large equipment, shovels, forklifts and sandbags – a vast field of sandbags. At first it appears chaotic, but after watching for a few seconds, patterns of activity begin to emerge. It reminds me of a nature film showing the inside of a beehive. At first it looks crazy, but it's soon clear that everything is being done in the most efficient manner possible. Which doesn't mean it's very neat. It's just *fast*. Now the television screen is showing scenes from various places along the river where the long flatbed trucks are delivering sandbags, and hundreds of volunteers have formed human chains, passing sandbags up and into place.

Many of them look like they're college age. Quite a few are younger. There's a few 30-to-40 year olds. But not too many fifty-plussers like me: After all, a sandbag chain can only go as fast as its slowest link. I'm still thinking about going anyway. But I haven't heard any more calls for sandbaggers like I did yesterday – in fact, there's been a few reports to the effect that so many volunteers have shown up today that the hundreds of buses now dedicated to transporting people to and from the places where they're needed are having trouble keeping up.

So maybe not today. I might just get in the way of all that youthful energy.

I sit down, transfixed by the scenes on the screen. It is one of the most remarkable scenarios I've ever taken in. And here's perhaps the most remarkable aspect of it: Almost everywhere, people are smiling. At Sandbag Central. On the sandbag lines along the river. Everywhere. They're working their buns off, sure. But there's a lot of chatting and smiling going on at the same time.

How could they not like each other? I think to myself. *What's not to like? How could they not feel good about what they're doing? What's not to feel good about? How could they not enjoy being with each other?*

It's been less than 100 hours since the forecast for the Red went from sort of lousy to near-apocalyptic. It occurs to me, watching these people, that true nobility has a humble face. And that heroes enjoy the company of their own kind.

Tuesday, March 24

We had nearly an inch of rain yesterday. And it's still coming down.

Kerstin is now saying that *over 10,000 volunteers showed up* at the various emergency centers yesterday, and the buses had trouble shuttling them all to and from the various sandbagging sights. Perhaps more than half of the volunteers were students, junior high through college.

The scene now changes to what's become a routine flood press conference every morning with Mayor Walaker. As we go to City Hall, it's just about to start. The mayor is coming into the room. I hadn't realized it before, but seeing him move through the sea of people, I realize he's another Viking. Lumbering up to the podium, he makes everyone he passes look pretty tiny – he must be at least 6'6", 300 pounds. He's not a clean-shaven

Viking like Tom and Jefferson, though. He wears a beard. It's well-trimmed, but it still makes him look even more Viking. All he needs is a helmet with horns and I'm certain the sun would break through the clouds over Fargo and strains of Wagner's *The Valkyrie* would begin ringing through the skies.

After straining to hear him talk for a moment, I turn the volume up on the TV. He's even more soft-spoken and low key than Tom and Jefferson. His words grumble as if they're coming up from the earth itself, falling out of an exceedingly relaxed face. I find myself thinking: *He's talking about saving Fargo, and he looks like he's almost falling asleep.*

Maybe he is almost falling asleep. He probably hasn't had much since last Thursday.

But listening to him speak for a minute, it's clear he's awake.

It's a question-and-answer press conference. Like most of us, he's heartened by the massive volunteer effort, but he's deeply concerned about the rain. It's not just the additional inch or more of rain – it's still falling as he speaks – that he's worried about, though. Yes, it could swell the Red perhaps another foot by itself. But there's another question: How much more of the water that's been frozen in the ground since last fall will the rain leach out? That's a harder question to answer, and it bothers him.

Over the last few days I've learned a lot more about our mayor. He worked for the city of Fargo for 32 years before being elected mayor three years ago. During the 1997 flood, he was

Operations Director for Fargo and managed that last great battle against the rising Red. When it comes to flood fighting, he knows what he's talking about. And people listen.

He may speak in a baritone sort of mutter, but he doesn't hold much back. In response to some question I don't hear well, he says that after the disaster of 1997, it took ten years for the economy of Grand Forks to recover to its former levels. But in the process, he says, that city managed to build, with state and federal help, a several-hundred-million dollar diked channel. So they, at least, are safe now. Fargo, however, which managed to save itself in 1997 through the heroics of a great number of its people, has no such channel, and no assurance of safety. If we are going to survive the looming waters of 2009, it seems, we'll need to pull off something of a miracle…

The phone rings. It's JoAnn Czerwinski, a neighbor. She says there's a meeting tomorrow night in the Reiles Acres Community Center for people who want to volunteer to help with the local flood-fighting effort.

"I'll be there," I say.

That was earlier today. Charlene and I are now watching the ten o'clock news. We learn the entire Red River Basin has had another inch of rain in the last 24 hours – a total of over two inches in the last two days. Then we see desperate scenes from the town of Crookston, Minnesota, about sixty miles away, shot earlier today. There hadn't been any evacuation planned, but people had to abandon their homes and flee the town when the

Red Lake River, a tributary of the Red that runs through Crookston, rose nearly four feet in just a few hours.

Something of a miracle, I hear Mayor Walaker saying as I try to fall asleep. *Something of a miracle.*

Wednesday, March 25

Now that the warming spell has done just about all the damage it can do, the weather's gotten cold again and it's begun to snow. Red River flood operations are on CNN now, and I'm seeing something I've never seen before: Evacuations from outlying areas – Abercrombie, Georgetown, Hickson, Oakport, Oxbow – are being done by airboat, the boats with the huge fans in the back that until this moment in my life, I've only seen whipping through hot, grassy marshes and swamps. Now they're whizzing across half-frozen lakes, seemingly oblivious to whatever surface is below them at the moment, moving effortlessly from flat ice into the river, then through eddies choked with spiky ice, and even up onto snow or soaked lawns at the edge of the floodwaters, taking evacuees aboard. Turns out these boats are just as handy in icy flood conditions as they are in marshes, for the same reasons: They have no propellers to get caught in anything, and the flat hull is excellent for traversing various wet surfaces, not just the grasses and quick sands of swamps, but also the wet, icy floodlands now overridden by the Red.

We're all over the national news today, the lead story everywhere. It's surreal watching Fargo flood operations on all the national broadcasts, and seeing those boats – boats I've only ever seen in swamps before – zipping all over the ice like floating snowmobiles through a steady snowfall, rescuing people from homes about to be engulfed by a Red River that is now, in some outlying areas, covering fields and neighborhoods miles beyond its banks. This, I know, is only the beginning. The crest isn't expected for a few more days. The national news organizations are all camped out here now, chattering excitedly with anticipation for an apex of disaster yet to be reached.

I hope we severely disappoint them. Another ten thousand mostly young volunteers have fanned out across the Fargo-Moorhead area again today, working their butts off to do just that. *That, at least, is one good thing that may come out of this*, I think. *People in other parts of the country are seeing a little of what the people around here are really like. Maybe it will begin to override that stupid fictional image everyone's had stuck in their heads since that goofy movie came out.*

I switch to local news coverage, which is better, because they cover what's actually happening on a minute-to-minute basis. I learn that Mayor Walaker said at the morning flood meeting we are now in "uncharted territory." That's significant, coming from the guy who successfully managed the 1997 flood effort.

170

A little before 7 p.m., I head over to the Reiles Acres Community Center for our local area flood meeting. Between explanations by Jefferson, our mayor, and a scientist neighbor by the name of Todd, I begin to understand, for the first time, the nature of the flood threat to our community.

Reiles Acres isn't directly threatened by the Red River – not *directly*. The Red is more than three miles to the east of us, with Hector International Airport and Interstate 29 elevating the intervening land more than enough to prevent overland flooding.

But less than two miles to our west lies the Sheyenne River, which flows into the Red about ten miles north of us. The trouble is, once the Red hits a little over 36 feet, which it's about to do, the Sheyenne stops flowing northward. Instead, the Red starts flowing southward, back up the Sheyenne, reversing its direction. At that point, the Sheyenne begins overflowing its banks, flooding the land for miles around.

That, I learn, is what happened back in 2006, when I'd so enjoyed the April sunsets reflecting off the waters covering the fields to our west. But that year, the Red had crested at a little over 37 feet. This year, it could go several feet higher. That could spell disaster for Reiles Acres.

Fortunately, Jefferson Bey is a very ahead-of-the-curve kind of mayor. He's had an earth-moving contractor putting a dike on the west side of Reiles Acres since March 20, one day after the National Weather Service dramatically elevated their crest forecast.

To the north, south and east, Reiles Acres is well protected from overland flooding by elevated roadways. But until now, the west side of our little community has been bordered by nothing but fields. That's why I'd been able to enjoy those watery sunsets in 2006 from our back deck. In the future, if I want to enjoy those sunsets during a spring flood, I'll have to walk down and climb to the top of our new dike.

As it turns out, that's the main point of this meeting. This is a new, hastily built dike, and it can't be trusted. When the water comes, it will have to be walked and watched 24 hours a day along its mile-and-a-quarter length until the water recedes. The smallest seepage or crack could quickly lead to a severe, possibly irreparable breach, turning our little community into a very cold version of Venice, Italy. So Jefferson is calling for volunteers to patrol the dike and send out an alarm for immediate repair at the first sign of anything amiss, starting tomorrow night, the earliest the water is expected to begin flowing into the fields to the west of us.

The dikes are dangerous, he warns. They're hastily and newly built, uneven and rugged along the top. They won't be easy to walk atop, which is what this patrol work calls for. "You'll have to watch your steps very carefully, especially at night, and you'll need to take a good flashlight and wear good climbing shoes or boots and warm clothing, because the forecast is for it to remain cold and snowy." Most dangerous, he says, there was no time to haul the clay from elsewhere. So running parallel along much of the eight-foot-high dike is an equally deep trench, from which the clay to build the dike was taken. Jefferson warns that a 16-foot fall from the top of the dike to the bottom of the trench awaits the first stumble or misstep. So there will always need to be a minimum of two people patrolling the dike at any one time, in case someone falls.

That said, we're free to sign up. An hour-by-hour calendar for the next two weeks is on a table in the middle of the main room of the community center, which will be flood watch central, open 24 hours a day, until the threat passes.

I want the surest-footed, most level-headed partner I know walking that dike with me. I tell Jefferson who that is. He understands and approves, as I thought he might, because he has a very similar member of his family. I immediately head home and tell Charlene everything I've learned. Then I say, "So I was thinking of asking Anastasia if she'd like to walk the dike with me."

"Yeah, that's what I was thinking," she says. "Sure. Go ahead and ask her."

I find Anastasia and repeat everything Jefferson said. "So would you be at all interested in walking the dike with me?" I ask.

"Yeah!" she says. No surprise. She has always delighted in taking on important, adult responsibilities, and shines at tackling them. She's a very physically aware, sure-footed athlete, to boot. I can't think of anyone less likely to fall into that trench – or who I'd rather have with me if I fall, which strikes me as a much more significant probability.

We walk the four houses back down to the community center to sign up. By the time we get there, though, the calendar is already pretty filled up. The nearest open spot left is Saturday, March 28th, from midnight to 3 a.m.

"Let's take that time, dad," Anastasia says to me. This doesn't surprise me, either – she's a night owl, and with school out, her schedule has already begun shifting nightward.

"Okay," I agree. I don't have any trouble staying up late, either. It's the nearest empty spot to the present, so by definition, it's the one Reiles Acres most needs. We sign up and head home.

It's just ten o'clock as we get back. I turn on the local news. In addition to the thousands of Fargoans devoting themselves to this already massive effort, a reporter is saying there are now people coming in from all over North Dakota and Minnesota – and some from as far away as Wisconsin, Montana, South Dakota and Iowa – to help with the sandbagging effort.

With the recent rains, snow and evacuations, things are more dire than ever. But looking at the screen, you wouldn't know it. Everywhere there are thousands of volunteers working tirelessly – and smiling. They're all smiling. And chatting. And working their buns off.

Jesus, I love this place. And that's not the least bit offensive. I think he'd like to hear it.

Thursday, March 26

At the morning flood meeting, the news is awful: The National Weather Service now says the Red could reach an all-time record 42-43 feet by the weekend. That's the highest projection yet, and well beyond the 112-year-old all-time record crest of 40.1 feet. I'm reminded again that the Grand Forks disaster 12 years earlier was precipitated by just such regular raisings of the projected crest for the Red.

Despite the miserable news, Walaker's bearing doesn't change. His voice still grumbles up out of the ground. He still looks resolute and half asleep at the same time. But for the first time, in his words there's an admission of the possibility of failure. "We want to go down swinging if we go down," he says.

It's the closest I've ever heard him come to saying we might not make it. It's a frightening development.

Perhaps that's what it's intended to be – although I doubt it. Walaker doesn't strike me as a calculating statement maker. He seems more like a guy who thinks about *how* he says things, not *what* he says – because *what* he says is always just what he already really thinks. Fargo. Very Fargo.

Looking out the front window of our house a little before noon, Anastasia and I notice a lot of activity going on around the Reiles Acres' utility shed, a large, nice looking building that houses the city's (yes, we're officially incorporated as a city) snowplow, lawnmower, truck and other large equipment. We decide to get bundled up – it's about 20 degrees out, with a fairly stiff wind blowing – and go see if there's something we can do to help.

We end up in the southwest corner of Reiles Acres, far from houses or roads, working with another neighbor, Bill Huber, to unhook a large firefighting-type hose that, until the freeze of the last day and a half, was conveying rainwater and snowmelt from that end of Reiles Acres out over the newly erected dike. But that hose is now frozen, and the pump is shut down. It takes about ten minutes of trying various things before we're able to unhook it from the pump it's frozen to. Then we begin digging it out of the ice and snow it's buried under along its 100-foot length. This takes us up and over the new dike. Anastasia and I pause atop the dike, huffing and puffing, and take a good look at it in the sunlight. This, after all, is where we'll be patrolling in the dark a couple of nights from now. Some patches, like the one we're on, look pretty smooth. The backhoe operator has had time to pack the top of the dike down fairly evenly, so it's easy to walk along the top here. But when we look north along the dike, we can see a decent little stretch that looks more like the Rocky Mountains, very jagged and uneven along the top. And that's also the stretch, we can see, where immediately alongside the dike is an 8-to-10 foot trench. It looks to me like about a 20-foot drop from the jagged top of the dike to the bottom of that trench, at about a 70 degree downward angle.

"The dike isn't rounded, like it would be if we had more time," I say to Anastasia, pointing at the rugged, peak-like stretch of dike to the north of us. "That's what we've got to climb over in the dark, unless one of the backhoe operators gets a chance to flatten the top of that stretch of dike there a bit before we patrol it in a couple of nights."

"Yeah, and there's that big trench right next to it," she says.

"You sure you want to do this at night?" I ask. "I can probably change to a later date, during the day."

"No, yeah, I'll be fine. Do *you* want to change?" She's looking at me now, slightly worried. She often makes me wonder who's more the parent.

"No, I'll be fine. You'll just have to fish me out if I fall in," I say, laughing.

"*Daaad*," she says, rolling her eyes. "Don't even say that."

"Maybe the backhoes will get a chance to pat down the top of the dike along there before Saturday," I tell her, "so it's more like this part when we walk it."

"Yeah," she affirms, cheerily.

About this time we realize that while we've been chatting for the last three minutes, Bill's been working hard trying to free the end of the hose stuck in the pond it created out in the field beyond the dike. We scramble down and help him finish the wet, cold, icy, mucky work. After another five minutes or so, we manage to free the final length of the hose from the frozen earth, ice and snow. The three of us together drag it up and over the dike, stopping to catch our breath once we make it back to the other end of the hose, the one we originally loosened from the pump.

After a brief discussion, Bill and I each take one of the ends of the hose, while Anastasia grabs the middle, and we begin hauling it across the snow and rugged terrain toward the Reiles Acres pickup truck waiting for us, about a hundred yards away. It weighs about a couple hundred pounds, I think, huffing and puffing as we drag it across the snow inefficiently, but the truck is now only about fifty yards away and I certainly don't feel like stopping to try and roll it up out here in the middle of the Reiles Acres tundra. We finally get it to the truck. The two men in the truck, who I recognize but don't know, climb out and take it from there, rolling it up and getting it into the bed.

We walk over to Bill's truck, which he drove us over here in, and climb in. He gives us a ride back to the Reiles Acres utility shed. By that time, activity seems to be winding down, and Anastasia and I walk home for lunch. We get out of our wet, icy clothes and fix ourselves some hot soup.

Turning on the local news, we learn that the people living in neighborhoods most vulnerable to flooding in the event of a breach in the dikes on either side of the Red – both in Fargo and Moorhead – are now being urged by city officials to evacuate, and assistance is being given to those who wish to leave.

By the time we finish lunch, all the earlier activity around Reiles Acres seems to have subsided. We both feel like taking a nap, but decide against it. Better to stay up as late as we can, then sleep in Friday morning. That night, we'll be walking the dike from midnight to 3 a.m. We'll want to be as wide awake as possible.

Watching the ten o'clock news, I learn that for the first time in it's 94-year history, MeritCare Hospital has decided to evacuate its patients, for two reasons: First, it would rather evacuate them under controlled circumstances rather than in the chaos following a breach in the dikes, and second, once evacuated, MeritCare will be in a much better position to help the many likely to need medical treatment in the event of a major levee breaking.

It's an economic and logistical nightmare for the hospital – and another unmistakable sign that we're teetering on the edge of complete and total disaster in Fargo. They wouldn't be doing this if they didn't think they had to.

And still, there are the same pictures on the screen following that story. Thousands and thousands of volunteers, mostly young, making sandbags, moving sandbags, putting sandbags in place.

And smiling.

I remember Adam, Brian, Gary and Nick, the young guys who didn't know us, but who helped us move into our new house here anyway, expecting nothing in return. I remember they emptied that huge moving van stuffed to the brim in half the time our well-seasoned driver said it could be done, damaging none of our belongings in the process.

I think about the river, moving inexorably upward, upward to levels never seen before.

I'm betting on Fargo, I say to myself as I finally fall asleep.

Friday, March 27

The river is still rising. I'm in the Hjemkomst Center, a tentlike structure adjacent to the Red in Moorhead that surrounds the authentic-style Viking ship *Hjemkomst,* built by Moorhead citizen Robert Asp in the 1970s, which his family sailed over 6,000 miles from Duluth, Minnesota to Norway in 1982. I'm standing next to the 75-foot long ship, positioned in the middle of the Center. It's pretty empty and quiet in here. Suddenly, I see water rapidly beginning to come in through the open glass doors at the back of the building, lapping across the polished floors.

People are rushing into the Center now. I look up at the ship and see Mayor Walaker wearing a round iron helmet with two horns protruding from the top. He looks almost as tall as the ten-foot dragon head rising from the bow of the ship behind him. He's barking orders at people, people I can't see who must be up in the ship with him. He is uncharacteristically animated. Suddenly, he looks directly down at me. "Come aboard!" he yells.

I do exactly as he says, jumping up and grabbing the top of the side of the boat and pulling my right leg over the top. As I bring my head up over the side of the ship I catch a glimpse of Jefferson Bey, the mayor of Reiles Acres, at the other end of the boat from Mayor Walaker, directing activity there. He seems to have some kind of helmet on too, but I didn't have time to see it well. Rolling over the side of the ship and falling between a couple of the oar benches on deck, I notice Tom, from the

Outdoorsman, across from me, not wearing a helmet, putting long oars through the slots in that side of the ship.

I wonder what these Vikings want me for. I feel tiny.

"Prepare to cast off!" Mayor Walaker bellows as more people desperately start climbing aboard the same way I just did. "Man the oars!"

Suddenly the tentlike roof far overhead begins to topple forward. The walls of the Center are washing away, the floodwaters rushing in. I get to my feet as water begins to hit the boat full force from behind. I stumble across the boat toward Tom, who effortlessly grabs my shoulder with one hand, keeping me from falling, and simultaneously spins me around so I'm suddenly facing the back of the boat as he guides me into a bench, his other hand holding an oar handle in position in front of me, all in a fraction of a second. "Row," is all he says, in his quiet, understated way. I grab the handle and start rowing like hell. At first, I row mostly air, but then I feel the water beginning to lift the boat off the floor of the Center, pushing it forward, the tentlike roof now lying in the river just ahead of us, completely toppled over, as the walls crumble completely away into the rushing water. We are now exposed to the elements, snow is falling, and because Tom has been filling the oar benches on this side of the boat, nearest the river's center, we're rowing toward deeper water. Many are still struggling to pull themselves aboard, soaked, while still others are completely immersed in the river now, swimming around us.

"Get the stragglers aboard!" I hear Mayor Walaker bellowing behind me. "Get the oars in reverse! We're not leaving anyone behind!"

I start rowing backwards. It's surprisingly easy. It's just pushing on the oar instead of pulling. Tom seems to have somehow gotten all the oarsmen – and women, I notice – in place, and with all of us rowing backwards, the *Hjemkomst* almost feels like its hovering in the air – in fact, I notice, the ship does seem to be lifting out of the water just a bit. No one is shouting a rowing cadence, we're all just naturally rowing in unison. Tom and Jefferson are now busy throwing rope ladders over the sides all around the perimeter of the ship, and dozens and dozens of people are climbing aboard.

And they're all *smiling*.

Everyone's aboard now, and everyone's smiling. Even Mayor Walaker's smiling. "Alright, oars forward," he says, no longer barking, his voice back to its normal low, raspy grumble. "Hold steady."

I pull back on my oar one last time, holding it steady, pointing it in the same direction it would be at the end of a full stroke. Everyone else is doing the same.

I can feel the bow of the ship lifting out of the water now, and I see the river below as… we… slowly… begin… to… fly.

The Red River Valley is spreading out beneath us now, and there's a lot of smiling and chit chat around me. *It's a happy little boat,* I think to myself as we sail upwards.

"Dad?" Austen's voice. I hear Austen's voice. I turn and see him standing next to me on the deck, concern in his eyes.

Oh, Jeez! "Where's Charlene and Anastasia?" I ask him, desperately looking around at all the people – hundreds of people, *thousands* of people – on board the ship, all smiling and chatting with one another. "Have you seen Char…"

"Dad?" I open my eyes. I'm laying in bed. Austen's standing over me.

"What, Austen?" I ask. I have to pee really bad.

"Is it okay if I have some spaghetti for breakfast?"

"Whoa," I say, thinking about the dream and rubbing my eyes.

"What's the matter?" Austen asks.

"Oh, I just had a really weird dream. I was flying on the Ark of Fargo."

"What?"

"I dreamt I was in a flying Viking ship with the mayor of Fargo," I tell him.

Austen laughs. "You are so weird, dad," he says, shaking his head.

"Excuse me," I say, getting out of bed and brushing past him toward the bathroom. "I have to pee."

"Can I have some spaghetti for breakfast?" he persists.

"That good leftover spaghetti from last night that mom fixed?" I ask as I sit down. When I'm barely awake, I sit down. It's safer.

"Yeah."

"Okay. Not too heavy on the noodles, though. Make sure you get plenty of chunks of meat in the sauce." I'm a believer in a high-protein breakfast.

"Okay," I hear him say, his voice trailing away as he trundles down the hallway toward the kitchen.

Out of the bathroom, I look at the clock. It's only 8:30 a.m. Anastasia and I stayed up until one in the morning, intending to sleep in, so we'd be well-rested for our midnight-to-three dike walk. Charlene knew the plan, but I forgot to tell Austen.

Oh well. *The cold and the danger will keep me awake*, I think, *even if I get a little tired by three in the morning.*

When I turn on the television, I learn that area schools have cancelled classes for all of next week. The North Dakota National Guard has taken control of a number of major streets, so the flatbed trucks carrying sandbags, as well as buses ferrying volunteers, don't have to battle traffic. Video of these streets, normally the busiest in town, is weird to watch. They're empty except for the occasional truck, bus or emergency vehicle. Some of the buses are now filled with people being evacuated to shelters that have been set up in higher areas that will remain safe, even if there's a major dike failure. The river is high enough now, approaching record levels, that any big break in a dike could quickly put large areas of Fargo about ten feet underwater, making it look the way New Orleans looked just three and a half years ago. That threat is keeping emergency jump teams busy, patching any leaks or small levee breaks wherever they appear.

I manage to take a nap around noon.

When I turn on the television in the afternoon, I learn the Red River has just surpassed it's 112-year-old record of 40.1 feet – and it's still rising. Then the news gets worse.

Federal officials have just recommended that Fargo be evacuated. If that's not a declaration we've lost, I don't know what is.

Then, a few minutes later, Mayor Walaker holds a press conference. I'm almost cringing as it begins, afraid I may be about to hear the worst.

But as I listen, I realize he's turning the whole thing around. He makes it clear that children and the elderly and the disabled should long since have left. But then he makes it equally clear that without the ten thousand-plus able-bodied Fargoans who have been fighting this battle, Fargo would have long since surrendered to the water. He says it would be crazy for them to leave now, throwing away the chance they've given Fargo with their remarkable work over the last week. They're why we're still here, and they're still the only hope we have of remaining intact through next week.

We don't want them to leave. *Of course* we don't want them to leave.

The Feds, I realize, are probably operating on complex formulae, telling them exactly under what conditions and contingencies a full evacuation ought to be recommended for any given community. The mayor, on the other hand, is operating on something else: Good common sense – or perhaps

– Good *Fargo* Sense. And in his best North Dakota Nice, he just told the Feds to stick it. He was so calm as he did it he might as well have been chatting about the latest baseball scores. It's almost a wonder he doesn't need a wheelchair to get around – he's clearly hiding cojones the size of watermelons somewhere.

As he finishes up his press conference, I suddenly hear myself yelling at the television screen:

*How **Fargo** of you! How Freaking **Fargo** of you!*

CHAPTER 11

More Sandbags to Heaven

Are we there yet?

2009 *continued*

Friday, March 27 *continued*

For the rest of the night, I can't stop thinking about Mayor Walaker's press conference. *If we make it out of this alive,* I keep thinking, *that will be the moment that defines this struggle. That will be the moment that* **saved** *Fargo.*

About 11:45, Anastasia and I get bundled up and drive down to the dike.

Saturday, March 28

It's just about midnight when we park at the westernmost end of our street, about thirty feet from the dike. We get out of the van.

"Hey, it's not too bad out," I say. "It's probably what? – about 25 degrees, I'd guess. Just a light breeze."

"Yeah, it's *nice*," Anastasia says in her cheery voice, making it sound like we're about to go for a morning stroll on a tropical beach.

"Well, yeah, compared to what it *could* be at the end of March, I suppose it *is* nice," I agree.

We have to trudge through a surprising amount of snow that's accumulated since we were out here Wednesday, lying in drifts between the end of the road and the dike. The area is well-lit by a streetlamp, and we walk around the largest drifts, about two feet high. Here, where 35th Avenue, the street our house is on, ends, there's no trench alongside the dike. We walk right up to it.

One of the two big backhoes Jefferson has had building this thing for the last week is now shut down and idle, less than fifty feet to the right of where we stand. The other is still working about a quarter-mile further down the dike, big lights on, shovel grinding noisily, still shoring up and packing.

The dike rises a good eight feet steeply in front of us. We begin climbing up the side. It's steep enough that we have to press our gloved hands to the side for balance as we go. We reach the top and stand. This is the mid-point in the dike – to our left, it runs about a half-mile south, then curves eastward, abutting the end of 32nd Avenue, Reiles Acres' southern border. To our right, it extends for just over a half-mile straight north, where it intersects with County Road 20, the northern end of Reiles Acres. About halfway to County Road 20 is where the one active backhoe is still noisily working away.

It's dark on the other side of the dike. We pull our flashlights out of our jackets and shine them at the base. The field below us is dry.

"Looks like the water hasn't made it this far yet," I say.

"Yeah. What about over there?" Anastasia points northwestward across the field. We shine our lights that way, but it's hard for me to see anything more than twenty feet from the dike. It's just too dark, and our flashlights aren't that powerful. What little I can see, however, looks dry.

"I don't know, Anastasia. I can't see anything out there. Can you?" She's got better eyes than I do, catlike eyes that see amazingly well in the dark.

"Maybe there's a little stream. I think I see something dark and glimmery about a half-mile away. I remember when the field got wet the last time, a stream came across the field from there first, and went down there" – her finger traces a line going kitty-corner across the field, until she's pointing southward down the dike. "Let's go that way first," she says, still pointing south. "The water first got close to the houses down there a couple of years ago."

"Okay," I say, tacitly acknowledging that her memory for her surroundings is better than mine, too. Plus, there's no backhoe working away down there. I'd rather not walk toward a big backhoe in action on a dark dike.

I start walking slowly southward along the top of the dike, slightly ahead of Anastasia, bearing to the left, the side the trench will be on. The terrain isn't too bad along this stretch. It's like the section of dike we stood on while we were moving that hose on Thursday. It occurs to me that we're now headed directly toward that part of the dike, and between here and there is where the clay resembled the Rocky Mountains. "Well, I guess we're about to see if one of the backhoes had a chance to flatten that spiky part of the dike we saw the other day," I say to Anastasia.

"Yeah, this part's pretty even here," she says, gingerly stepping around a loose chunk of clay about one-foot in diameter with her effortless skater's grace.

"Wait a second," I say, stopping and putting my right arm out. She stops just behind and to my right.

"I just want to stop and see if we can see what's ahead," I say. "I don't want to try looking ahead while we're walking." I take my light off the ground immediately before us and point it forward into the dark. Anastasia does the same. It's like a couple of minutes ago, when we peered out into the field. I just can't see much beyond twenty feet or so – but what little I can see looks like the dike is about to get a lot more rugged. "The top of dike looks pretty rough ahead," I say, "but I'm not sure if it's as bad as it was the other day."

"Yeah, maybe they got to do a little work on it," Anastasia says.

"We'll see when we get there, I guess. I want to look around for a second." I shine my light along the side of the dike adjacent the field.

"It still looks dry," Anastasia says.

"Yeah." I shine my light on the other side of the dike. "Whoa!" I say, looking about twenty feet nearly straight down into a chasm I hadn't realized was there. "We're right above the trench they dug to build the dike already."

"Yeah," Anastasia says, shining her light down into the depths. "That's really deep."

"You okay?" I ask, hearing the caution in her voice. Actually, that's one of the reasons I liked the idea of walking the dike with her – I knew I'd be more cautious, so as not to freak her out. Even in dangerous situations, I can daydream, sailing off to *Planet Marc* unexpectedly. I knew I wouldn't if she was with me.

"Yeah," she says, "I'm fine." We shine our lights along the trench, paralleling the dike for as far ahead as we can see. We were about five feet past where the trench started. We'd been so focused on the terrain on top of the dike immediately before us – as we should be – we hadn't noticed the land dropping away to our left.

"I want us to stay on the right side of the dike," I tell Anastasia. "Until we see water, that's where we should be focused, anyway. If we see any water on that side, then we'll have to start looking for leaks or seepage on the Reiles Acres' side. But until then, we'll just try to stay to the right."

"That makes sense," Anastasia says, boosting my confidence. She's smart and honest enough I know she won't say anything like that to *anyone* – least of all a male member of her family – unless what they've said *really does make a lot of sense*.

"Okay, let's go," I say, shining my light on the ground immediately in front of us and beginning to move forward once again.

The terrain gets more rugged quickly. Soon we're having to step up a foot here, slide down a couple of feet there. Every ten or twenty feet we stop and shine our flashlights down along the base of the dike. Still no water.

About five minutes into this Rocky Mountain section of the dike, we have to step over a large crack about six inches wide running through the top. "Okay, we'll need to report this when we get back," I tell Anastasia. After stepping over the crack, we stop and turn around. I shine my light down into it. It looks at least a foot deep.

"Okay. There's no water here yet, anyway," she says, shining her light out into the field.

"I can see about a good foot down into this thing," I say, still shining my light into and along the crack. "And the separation could go a lot further, maybe even all the way down."

"Oooh, yeah," Anastasia says, shining her light into the crack now.

"Anyway, the dike is clearly separating here, that side's going that way and this one's going the other, so we'll need to report it so they can get a backhoe over here to fix it before any water arrives. Where are we?" I stand up and look over at Reiles Acres. I see we're about an eighth of a mile from where we started.

"We're almost directly in line with that street," Anastasia says, pointing over to a street that ends about a hundred yards away from where we're standing. "It's the next street down from ours, where we parked," she observes.

I scan the block between the street we're lined up with and our van, which shines brightly under a streetlight we parked near. "Yeah, you're right. It's probably Thirty-Fourth Avenue. We should check it just to make sure when we get back in the van. Then we'll go to the Community Center and report it or leave a big note before we drive out to County Road Twenty. We won't have to walk the dike from County Road Twenty unless we see water."

"Yeah, I remember," Anastasia says. I had explained our basic route when I first asked if she wanted to join me.

"The dike out there is built up over an older dike, Jefferson said, so if we have to walk it, it should be a lot smoother than this, at least."

"That's good," Anastasia says.

"But if we don't see any water when we get out there, we'll drive further west on County Road Twenty until we come to water, so we can see how close it's getting and report that."

"Okay."

"Alright, you ready?"

"Yeah," Anastasia says, cheery voice intact. She starts off ahead of me now, clambering up some yard-square chunks of clay dropped by a backhoe that had clearly been in too much of a hurry to take the time to pack them down smoothly before digging the next huge shovelful out of the trench below.

After another twelve minutes or so of traversing this rugged stretch of dike, the terrain starts evening out and we can walk again, stepping around the occasional large clod. A few minutes later, we make it down to the area of the dike where we had stood a day and a half ago. "There's a little water down there with the snow," Anastasia says, shining her light on the field below, "but I'm not sure if that's the same water we saw on Thursday, the water that got pumped out before the pump froze."

"If it is, I think it would be frozen by now," I speculate. "But some of it still looks wet. How warm did it get today?"

"I'm not sure," Anastasia says. "I think it got kind of warm. It was pretty sunny."

194

"Alright, well, either way, it doesn't look any deeper than it did, maybe just six inches or so."

We check both sides of the dike with our flashlights. Unlike the section with the newly dug trench, this area still has lots of snow on the ground. It occurs to me there might be a little water running underneath that snow.

"I just need to check something really fast," I tell Anastasia, quickly climbing down the Reiles Acres side of the bank. This is an old section of dike, created, for some reason unknown to me, a long time ago – so it's smooth and rounded, and easy to get up and down.

When I reach the bottom I kick the snow around in a few places looking for water. None.

"Alright, no water there," I say, climbing back up the dike.

"Let's keep going," Anastasia says, heading south again. The dike is starting to curve eastward now, in toward Reiles Acres. Looking ahead, I can see where the dike abuts 32nd Avenue.

"Okay," I say, getting back to the top of the dike and following. "But if the field gets dry we'll turn around and head back to the van. Then we'll go down to Thirty Second Avenue and walk the dike from that direction before we go to the Community Center. And we'll double check that street across from the crack we found in the dike and make sure it's Thirty-Fourth Avenue."

"Okay. Well, the land's dry here already," she says, shining her light along the field side of the dike about fifteen feet in front of me. "Let's go back."

The return trip along the dike is uneventful. We get back to the van. The clock says 1:22. We drive over to confirm that the street lining up with the crack in the dike is 34th Avenue – but it isn't. It's where 34th Avenue ought to be, but instead, the street signs tell us, it's Bakers Lane.

Then we drive down to 32nd Avenue and park at its westernmost point, where it ends and the dike begins. We climb up the dike and walk until we arrive, once again, at the spot where we were when we helped Bill retrieve that big hose on Thursday. Once again, that's the only place we see any water.

"I think that water probably is the same water that was here a couple of days ago, dad," Anastasia says.

"Yeah, just the water that got pumped out through the hose we hauled, during the rainy days before the pump froze."

We head back to the van, drive to the Community Center and go inside. The appointment book with the dike walking schedule is still on the center table where it was the other night when we signed up. The Center's empty, but there are cookies and coffee and hot chocolate that we help ourselves to, while I write a quick note about the crack in the dike we found.

"Okay," I say as I sign the note, "Let's drive out to County Road Twenty."

We get back in the van and head down to 45th Street, which runs along the east side of town. We turn left and drive a little more than a half-mile north to County Road 20, where we turn left and head toward where the dike meets the road at a 90 degree angle, about a half-mile ahead.

On the right side of the road up ahead we see a flashing yellow light, about the right height to be atop a good-sized pickup truck.

"What's that?" Anastasia asks.

"I'm not sure," I answer. "It looks like it's right across from where the dike should be." As we get closer, I can see it's atop the cab of a truck parked on a side road just a short distance past the dike. "I bet that's the Reiles Acres truck," I say, driving past the dike and slowing down a couple hundred yards before we reach the truck with the flashing yellow light atop the cab. "I bet there's someone else out tonight, too."

Sure enough, it's the city's big pickup truck. I pull onto the side road alongside it and lower my window. The driver's side window of the pickup truck, now just a couple of feet from mine, lowers at the same time, revealing... *Wally!*

"Hey, Wally," I say, all enthusiasm. "What're you doing out here?" Wally is married to JoAnn, the lady who'd called to tell me about the flood prep meeting in the first place. He does most of the snowplowing and other tough jobs around Reiles Acres, while still working for the railroad full-time. Imagine Wilfred Brimley twenty years younger, a foot taller and with a hundred pounds less fat and fifty pounds more muscle, all containing a wickedly wry, dry, pointed Midwestern wit. That's Wally, sort of an upper Eastern European Viking type. About fifty or so, I think Wally's somehow managed to work for the railroad since they put the first line across the country the century before last, and he knows and has practiced just about everything about how anything that's down-to-earth enough to really mean something needs to be done if you want to really get everything done *right*.

I always like seeing Wally.

As his driver's side window comes all the way down, however, I see that Wally's not all smiles in return. "What're you doing out here?" He's asking the same question I just asked him, not bothering to answer mine. I can see there's another man, who I don't recognize off the top of my head, in the passenger's seat.

"We're patrolling the dike," I say, still smiling. Wally's the kind of guy who can look really angry while he says something just to get you on edge before he cracks up. I think that might be what's going on here. *Okay, I'll play along.* "We're scheduled from twelve to three tonight."

"Did you sign in?" he asks, still unsmiling.

"No… I never heard anyone say anything about signing in." Wally still isn't smiling. I'm beginning to get the idea, and think it might be wise to let him know what we'd been doing the last hour and a half. "We got out a little before midnight and walked the southern half of the dike. Found a pretty big crack in the top of it about where it lines up with Thirty-Fourth Av… uh, I mean, Bakers Lane, and left a note in the Community Center about it and got some coffee," – I raise my little Styrofoam cup in sort of a toast – "and then headed out here. We're going to look for water and walk the dike if any's gotten that far. Otherwise we were going to drive down and see how close the water's getting now."

"Got flashlights?" Still no smile.

"Yeah," Anastasia and I answer in unison, like troops to a sergeant, both holding up our flashlights for Wally to see.

"Those aren't flashlights," Wally says, holding up a big Maglite, "That's a flashlight."

"Oh."

"Got your Reiles Acres badges on?"

"Didn't know there was such a thing."

"Wearing your orange vests?"

"Apparently not."

"Are you driving the Reiles Acres' truck?"

"Uh… Doesn't look like it," I say, looking at the Reiles Acres logo on the door of the Reiles Acres truck that Wally's sitting behind the wheel of. I'm gleaning that Wally is not happy about how this whole *patrol the dikes* thing has been whipped together. And I can tell by the look on his face that he probably doesn't think highly of a fourteen-year-old girl being on dike patrol. *If he only knew,* I think to myself, *she's the really dependable one.*

There's a brief pause in the line-of-fire questioning, so I decide to throw in a question of my own. "So I suppose you've already been down the road and seen where the water is now?"

"It's right over there," Wally says, pointing to the next side road west. "The water's just starting to come into the field now." The side road he's pointing to is slightly lit by the outside lights of a farmhouse just beyond it, and squinting, I think I make out a sliver of dark, reflective surface coming over the roadway and into the field – right at the point where, an hour ago, Anastasia said she saw it.

It suddenly occurs to me what must've happened. "So I bet you were out of town on railroad work when this whole dike patrol was set up," I say.

"Yep," Wally says with a single nod.

"Ah." I nod back, single nod. I can see Wally's relaxing just a bit with that. *At least the dumb...ss gets that much*, I can kind of hear him thinking. (Hey, I'm not arguing... When it comes to the stuff Wally's good at, I'm no genius.)

"Well, let's get back to the Community Center and get you guys set up right," Wally says, putting his truck in gear.

"Okay, we'll be right behind you," I say, pulling forward so Wally can see to his left before pulling out. I notice the road we're on only goes about ten feet before it drops off into the field, so after Wally turns onto County Road Twenty, I back out onto the otherwise deserted road and follow.

Boy, I'm kinda glad that didn't happen before I had that Fargo Ark dream, I think to myself on the way back. *If it had, Wally probably would have been in that boat chewing me a new *ss*ole – or throwing me overboard.*

Back in the Community Center, Wally's partner introduces himself and tells us where his house is located in town, all of which stays in my head for a good half-second or so. Then he shows us where to sign in and get our badges, orange vests and Maglites. I glance up at the clock on the wall. It's now almost 2:30. Wally's already found the note I've written about the crack in the dike and asks me a few questions about it. "Okay, I'll get this to Jefferson so he can get a backhoe out there tomorrow to fix that up," he says. Then he gives me the keys to the Reiles Acres truck and tells me how to drive it. *C'mon Wally, I'm not that hopeless, am I?* I think to myself. *It's even an automatic for cry-sakes.* Wally tells us we don't need to walk the dike any more, just drive around one more time to the two ends of the dike, where it meets 32nd Avenue and County Road Twenty, and see if anything has changed, then come back.

We do exactly as he says. We get back about ten minutes before three. One of our replacements, Brian Smith – a wonderful realtor (now there's a phrase I never spoke before coming to North Dakota) who sold us our home here – is already there, waiting for his dike-walking partner and chatting with Wally and the guy whose name I can't remember. After returning the keys, vests, badges and Maglites, Anastasia and I check the patrol schedule. There aren't any open slots for the next week. "We'll probably be done by then," Wally says, nursing a cup of coffee. He looks tired. And maybe a bit relieved that Anastasia and I have probably just completed our one-and-only dike walk.

"You look like you should go home and get some sleep, Wally," I tell him.

"I will, after the sun comes up," he says. It's clear he's got to make sure everything gets done right, at least until the light of day, when there will be lots of eyes able to see what's going on.

It's good to know Wally is around. I suspect that if not for the Wallys among us (although there's really no one else quite like *Wally*), Fargo would have been underwater a few days ago.

Anastasia and I head home, ready to crash, but find ourselves still pretty revved. We stay up almost until five in the morning watching some goofy thing on television before finally heading off to bed.

About noon I wake up and fix something to eat. I turn the television on and hear the best news I've heard in weeks: The Red River may have crested! It's set a new all-time record – 40.82 feet – but it may be beginning to head back down.

Fargo has to remain vigilant – we're still just one major levee break away from a terrible disaster. *But the river may have stopped rising.* It's the most hopeful thing we've heard in the nine days since March 19, when the National Weather Service first said, "Oh, and by the way… you have a disaster coming in less than a week. Have a Nice Day!" (Alright, that's not very Fargo of me… but if we're being honest, that's how it felt. Oh, gee, *thanks for letting us know…*)

But the river may have stopped rising.

On the heels of this good news, however, we get yet another lovely forecast: A new storm could dump eight inches of snow on us in the next few days.

Still, *we may be winning.*

202

Sunday, March 29

During the night, a section of the permanent flood wall at Oak Grove Lutheran School failed.

*I know those flood walls. I've seen and touched those flood walls. Those are... **were**... some heavy duty flood walls.*

I watch a live video feed of a National Guard helicopter lowering a huge sandbag into the breach to stem the inrushing river. But it's not in time to save the school from yet another severe flooding, like the one they underwent in 1997.

It's unsettling to watch the disaster unfolding on their campus, knowing how strong their new flood walls were – and knowing that 90 percent of the dikes and levees that nearly a couple hundred thousand people are now depending on – depending on for nearly everything material they own – are made of much flimsier stuff.

The river is down from its crest, though.

But the storm is coming.

Monday, March 30

The snowstorm first forecast a couple of days ago has hit, and it's a howler. It's not a blizzard – there's not enough snow to make it one, thank goodness – but it's packing 30 mile-per-hour winds. *Great, that's just what miles of sandbag levees need*, I think, *lots of big waves on the water.*

Hundreds of volunteers, mostly people who live along the river and know it well – and whose houses are literally on the front lines – are helping the National Guard patrol the levees, looking for the slightest weaknesses and shoring them up. Other than that, though, video from around town is eerily quiet. No one's driving anywhere, except the occasional emergency or National Guard vehicle. No one's walking anywhere. No one's at work. No stores are open. And no one's sandbagging – there's now a surplus of sandbags in the Fargodome and various emergency outposts around town.

Like almost everyone else, we're staying home today.

Tuesday, March 31

We wake up to a newly white world. Ten inches of snow descended on us, mostly overnight. It's worrisome, because it, too, will melt, probably soon, adding water to the river.

But the river is now below 38 feet! If it keeps going down, this latest ten inches of snow may be insignificant.

Some of the people who evacuated a few days ago are coming back. A few of the national newscasters are saying what a remarkable story it is that Fargo has survived by its wits and its will. Local news people, however, know better. We haven't survived yet. There's optimism, sure – but it's guarded.

April 2009

Wednesday, April 1: Businesses in Fargo and Moorhead are allowed to reopen. That's the first sign that it's for real: We may have made it.

Meanwhile, there's a little water in the fields to the west of Reiles Acres now, I hear. Can't see it, though. Our new dike is blocking my view and it's doing just fine, I understand. No more occasional watery sunsets from my back deck, I guess. Oh, well. There are advantages and disadvantages to everything, a very bright philosopher once told me.

Thursday, April 2: I see video of people I know up in Harwood, a few miles north of us, having to take a boat across a few hundred yards of flooded roads to get to work. Their houses are apparently okay, but their neighborhood is now an island. So some of the residents have started a little volunteer ferry service. *How Harwood of them.*

Friday, April 3: The National Weather Service has just predicted another crest *at least as high as the last one – maybe higher.*

Then Mayor Walaker says, in his North Dakota Nice way, that it ain't gonna happen. The National Weather Service is, simply put, wrong.

He's been watching the Red for three decades, he explains. He's been out looking around the Basin the last couple of days, he explains. He knows the data the National Weather Service is basing their prediction on, he explains. But they're wrong, he explains. They should know better, too, he explains. People should have a relaxing weekend, he explains.

I believe him. So does everyone else I talk to.

Saturday, April 4: The Red is now below 35 feet. Hard to imagine the Mayor's not right.

Sunday, April 5: Down to 34 feet. The river would now have to rise more than 6½ feet back up for the National Weather Service to be right.

Monday, April 6: The kids are back to school, Char and I are back to work. A number of volunteers and city workers are now busy raising and reinforcing levees, preparing for the Red to rise again, which everyone knows it will. But still, no one I've heard thinks it will get back over 40 feet. Everyone thinks the Mayor knows what he's talking about.

Tuesday, April 7: Now even the National Weather Service says the Mayor's right. Not that they put it that way. The revised prediction is for a second crest between 38 and 40 feet in another 9-11 days.

April 8-15: The Red got down below 33 feet before it started to rise again, never making it back up past 36 feet. Guess the National Weather Service was all wet. Volunteers in Fargo and

Moorhead have produced and placed more than 3 million sandbags, surpassing Mayor Walaker's original call by more than a full million.

But the real story this week was the Sheyenne River, the one that runs a couple miles to the west of Reiles Acres before it flows into the Red. It's not been a story for us here – now that the Red's below 36 feet, the Sheyenne is coming back under control. But it turns out the Sheyenne crosses about half of North Dakota before it gets here – and much of that half of the state got even more snow than we did in the last days of March. All that snow melted almost immediately, engorging the Sheyenne along much of its route. The largest population affected is in Valley City, a town of nearly 7,000 about 60 miles west of Fargo, where the Sheyenne just crested at nearly 22 feet, a full two feet higher than the previous record of 20 feet set over 125 years ago, in 1882. Much of Valley City – as well as more than a dozen smaller towns along the Sheyenne – has been evacuated.

April 16-23: Valley City has survived, but just barely. A sewer failure caused by pressure from the Sheyenne caused more evacuations, and they had to bring in 200 porta-potties – the whole darn town had to use porta-potties! But like the rest of North Dakota, they've now survived the worst flood season on record.

In the process, the world has gotten a brief glimpse of what *Fargo* really means. I guess there's a bright side to everything.

*   *   *

2010

Thursday, April 22

The flood fight this year turned out to be nowhere near last year's titanic struggle, thank goodness. After my conversation with Tom at the *Outdoorsman* last month, I really wanted to go out sandbagging. At that time, mid-March, we still didn't know how bad it might get. First, I decided I better make an appointment for myself with my daughter's chiropractor, Dr. Brook Townley (who literally worked wonders with Anastasia a couple of years ago when more conventional methods had completely failed to solve debilitating headaches she'd started experiencing a few months earlier). When I asked her if she thought I could do some sandbagging, the good doc asked me a lot of questions. Then she decided to take some X-Rays. Then she gave her verdict: "You can volunteer to bake the Rice Krispy treats."

She's almost as smart-ass as I am. *I think I love her, in a Fargo sort of way.* And since the treatments that followed that first appointment, my left shoulder feels much better than it has in many months, too. *Thanks, Doc.*

Turns out, there weren't that many volunteers needed this year anyway, even though the Red got up past 30 feet (18 feet is flood stage). That's because, starting in late April of last year, along with going to Washington to push for help on a permanent solution to what appears to be Fargo's continually increasing flood problem, Mayor Walaker, along with Mayor Voxland of Moorhead, began preparing for the flood of 2010 *about ten months ahead of time*. So instead of having only five days to produce two million sandbags, there were already nine months of preparation behind them by the time the Red started rising in 2010. As a result, city authorities and officials were able to handle almost everything needed by themselves this year.

That was extremely Fargo of these officials. But it also makes me wonder: Is this how a powerful sense of community begins to dissipate as a metropolis grows? I understand the wisdom and necessity of better preparations and, as soon as possible, a full-fledged diversion, so the safety of the urban core of our region is assured for the foreseeable future. But as we relegate our survival functions to specialists, we inevitably have less reason to come together, and more reason to focus on our own, individual specialties and concerns.

This morning I bought a copy of the book *Will Over Water*, a blow-by-blow recounting of last year's flood fight put together by the Forum newspaper and WDAY news. It's a big, coffee-table sized book with lots of great photos.

William C. Marcil, the publisher of the Forum, writes in the opening sentence of *Will Over Water*: "The cover says it all." The cover is a nearly life-sized photo of the mud-splattered face of 12-year-old Zach Boor as he hoists a sandbag into place.

Marcil does some fine writing on that first page: *The people were exhausted, but they laughed. They were dirty, but they smiled. They were concerned, but determined. They thought: If anybody can beat Mother Nature, we in the Red River Region can.*

Will Over Water gives me just what I need: A straight-forward account of what happened each day, from the beginning of the flood fight to its victorious end. Now I have a skeleton on which to hang my personal recollections.

But after reading through it, I have a problem.

The singular moment that most represents the flood fight for me is completely missing. Nada. Nowhere. Not there.

That's weird, because it was arguably one of the two or three most newsworthy events of the entire flood fight.

So I get out the DVD included in the book, a blow-by-blow summary of the newscasts done by WDAY during that same period. Surely the single most important defining moment of the flood fight – of the *Fargoness* of it all – will be included somewhere there.

Nope. Nada. Nothing.

How can this be?

In desperation, I look at the Acknowledgements on the back page of the book. There's a big group photo with a caption that reads: *The Forum's Flood Coverage Team,* followed by the names of all the people in the photo. I look at the three dozen people standing in a large printing room. One of the smiling faces in the front row immediately pops out at me. It's the face of someone who listens, and someone who's fun to talk to. *That's the face of someone who knows everyone who knows everything*, I think to myself. She's the third person from the right in the front row. I count back three names from the end and find hers: Stephanie Selensky.

I look up the number for the Forum Newsroom and call.

"Forum newsroom," comes a nice voice.

"Hi, is Stephanie Selensky available?" I ask.

"Sure, I'll put you through."

"This is Stephanie," comes a cheerful voice to match the photo.

"Hi, Stephanie, my name's Marc de Celle and I've got kind of a weird question. I have a problem I hope you can help me with."

"Okay, I'll see what I can do." *Jeesh. I haven't even told her what it is yet, and she already says she'll see what she can do. This lady's Fargo. Very Fargo. Jackpot.*

"Great. Here's my problem. I'm writing a book about Fargo, and I'm trying to write a chapter about the flood fight last year. It's just a first-person, personal, human-interest kind of a book, nothing technical, but I needed a reference for what happened when, so I went down this morning and bought a copy of *Will Over Water*."

"Oh, yeah."

"And it's great, exactly what I need, except for one thing."

"What's that?"

"Well, the moment that most defined the flood fight for me last year – do you remember when the National Weather Service or FEMA or some other federal agency recommended that Fargo be evacuated?"

"Oh, yeah. Sure."

"And then Mayor Walaker held a press conference about five minutes later and said, 'Look, sure, all the young children and the elderly and disabled should have been out of here a long time ago, but the only reason the town's not already ten feet underwater is because something in excess of ten thousand able-bodied volunteers have kept the town from going underwater, and we'd be crazy to ask these people to leave...'"

"Oh, yeah, sure, I remember that."

"Well, it's not in your book."

"Oh."

"And I'm guessing it's a *North Dakota Nice* thing," – Stephanie starts chuckling as soon as I say this – "and the reason it's not in your book is 'Why should we stick the federal government's nose in it if we don't have to?' —especially when we need to be working with these people over the next few years to try get some kind of a decent diversion built before the next time Mother Nature tries to temporarily turn us into Lake Agassiz around here again."

"Well," Stephanie says, still chuckling, "we don't really base our editorial policies on North Dakota Nice."

"Hmmm. Well, that was just my guess," I said, "because I couldn't figure out any other reason that the seminal moment of the entire flood would be completely missing from an otherwise excellent account." I suddenly realized I'd better not dwell on this mysterious conundrum or I'd end up never getting what I needed. "Anyway, Stephanie, I need to know what day that happened, because for me, that was the moment that defined the whole thing. So when I couldn't find it in your book I looked at the picture in the back under the Acknowledgements and I saw your smiling face in the front row I thought you looked like the person who knows everyone who knows everything" – she was chuckling again now, *good sign* – "so I was hoping you might be able to help me find out what day it was when the Feds told us to evacuate and the mayor said, in so many words, 'well, pardon me for butting in here, but, **NO.**'" Another chuckle. "Or if you could at least tell me who you think I should call who'd be able to help me."

"Sure," came her cheery voice back, still chuckling a little, "I'll just look in the records here first and see what I can find and call you back, okay?"

"Thanks, Stephanie, that would be wonderful."

Then she asked for my phone number and we said goodbye.

So now I'm fixing a snack. It's only been a couple of minutes since my call so I figure I've got some time on my hands. Maybe I'll go see if there's a game on televi...

The phone is ringing. The caller ID says FORUM. Wow. That wasn't even five minutes.

"Hello?"

"Hi. Is this Marc?"

"Yeah, hi, Stephanie. Boy, that was fast."

Chuckle. "Well, I looked up the stories from those days and it happened before March 29, because that's the first day the stories refer to federal authorities recommending an evacuation and the mayor responding."

She reads me a couple of brief excerpts from the stories she's looked up, confirming what she just told me.

"Does it say who ordered the evacuation?" I ask. "I mean, was it FEMA, or the National Weather Service or…"

"It just says 'federal officials'" she says.

"Okay, great, Stephanie, that's exactly what I needed. Thanks *so much*."

"Good luck with your book."

"*Thanks*, Stephanie."

*   *   *

Fargo sits near the southern end of what was, about ten thousand years ago, the largest freshwater lake on the planet, Lake Agassiz. This immense body of water took up more area than all the modern Great Lakes, and held more water than all the freshwater lakes in the world today, combined.

Fed by glacial runoff at the end of the last Ice Age, several controversial studies suggest that when, about 8,000 – 10,000 years ago, it finally broke through huge ice dams bordering it to the north, so much water may have poured into the Atlantic so fast that a surge rippled around the world's oceans, causing many of the ravaging floods recorded in almost every ancient text – including the Bible.

Or it may have just trickled out under those dams for centuries. Either way, Lake Agassiz is gone.

The world changes. It always does. And someday, despite the better efforts of mice and men and even great leaders, Fargo will not be as it is today.

If I'm still in this world, and those changes are mainly physical changes, I won't care that much, to be perfectly honest. Because for me, Fargo is no longer a place. It's not the flat clay plains left by glaciers crushing the middle of North America before melting away, or the old downtown being revitalized with high-tech money. I'll be happy, wherever I am, as long as I'm surrounded by the kind of people I've found here, who have so often given me occasion to say, from the bottom of my heart:

How Fargo of You.

CHAPTER 12

The Fly, the Wind and the Windshield

No splat!

Our first month living in Fargo, I noticed the flies were different around here. They looked the same as flies in other places. But they acted differently. *Very* differently. They're sort of... well, apologies to funk great Curtis Mayfield, but they're sort of *superflies*.

Regardless of where you live, if you leave one of your car windows open overnight and a fly or two happens to have spent the night rent-free in your garage, you may hear that lovely buzzing sound first thing in the morning. You know, you're not that awake yet, you've just managed to get your coffee into the cup holder and seat belt on, go to turn the key and... bzzzzzz. Right by your ear. Now he's eyeing your coffee. He's probably got some awful month-old muck from inside your garbage can stuck between his little taste bud toes. (Yes, flies have taste buds on their feet.)

You shoo the little bugger away just before he lands on the lip of your coffee cup. You need that coffee. But he's still buzzing. Threatening. *Irritating.*

Back in Arizona, California and Florida, this was easy to solve: Open a back window. *Whoosh* – the fly was gone. As soon as you got up to twenty miles an hour or so with a back window open, there weren't any flies capable of resisting that kind of airflow. Sucked right out. I mean, if it was a big ol' horsefly, maybe I had to open one of the front windows just a crack. But that was an extreme measure seldom needed.

Lowering a window might be mildly inconvenient on a 110º summer day, when I'd rather not open a window at all. But that was the extent of it: a brief inconvenience.

So one morning during our first month here – August 2005 – when I got into the van and heard lots of buzzing, I didn't think much of it. I'd left the garage doors open late the day before for maybe an hour, then left some of the windows to the van open overnight. Oh well. I'd just leave the windows open and by the time I drove the quarter-mile down 35th Avenue heading out of Reiles Acres, I'd be fly-free.

Didn't happen. By the time I got to 45th Street and turned north, I still had several flies buzzing around inside the van. I wasn't sure I'd even lost one fly yet. Fifteen miles an hour clearly wasn't going to do the trick.

Hmmm, I thought to myself, *these little buggers are adapted to the wind up here.*

*   *   *

North Dakota is the windiest state in the nation. That's not a guess. Increasing interest in wind power over the last decade led to a spate of national studies confirming it. There are now lots of plans in the works for wind farms to grace the Northern Prairie around these parts. One of the country's most successful wind-tower manufacturers, DMI Industries, is based here.

The wind has lessons. Lessons that may teach us a little about why this part of the country is the way it is. The flies were to show me this. One fly in particular.

*   *   *

By the time I reached the last stop sign on the way out of town, I'd lowered all the windows in the van. All the way down.

Ahead of me was a good half-mile of paved road, nothing but fields on either side. I took off.

Twenty. No sign of fly distress. They not only weren't being *whooshed* out, they were still buzzing around inside, going wherever they pleased, just as if the van were standing still! *I didn't know there were any flies that could do that*, I thought to myself. I stepped on the gas a little more.

Thirty. It was still a happy little fly party. One of them landed on a little spot of soda one of the kids had spilled on the carpet the other day, then got up and casually buzzed over to a piece of potato chip wedged in the seat. The wind wasn't affecting their little fly buffet *at all*. If anything, they seemed, perhaps, a little more energized. *Do they actually like the wind?* I wondered.

I pushed harder on the accelerator. I caught a glimpse of my hair in the rear view mirror whipping around Einstein-like. The flies, however, were still engaged in fully controlled flight patterns. They seemed to be staying a little closer to the van's inner surfaces than before – I didn't see any of them blithely cruising by an open window as they'd been when I was only going twenty. But still, I didn't seem to be losing any of them out of any of the open windows yet, either.

This is amazing, I thought to myself. And then I started to hear it. The taunting. Slowly getting louder, making its way into my consciousness... Squeaky little fly voices, whizzing all around:

"He's trying to blow us away, man!"

"Yeah, buzz his head! Ha ha ha."

"Wing his nose while you're at it!"

Followed by lots of squeaky little fly laughter.

I started trying to shoo them out of the van. They dodged my hand, then suddenly were gone.

Finally, I thought. I looked at the speedometer. *I'm doing over fifty*, I realized with amazement.

Then I looked up and slammed on the brakes just in time to come to a screeching halt a few inches past the stop sign at County Road 20. *Man, shooing flies in North Dakota can be as dangerous as driving drunk!* I sat at the stop sign for a while, waiting for my racing heart to settle. No other cars in sight. Thankful for that.

I looked around. No flies in sight. I pulled onto County Road 20, heading the half-mile east to the freeway. I started putting the windows up.

Bzzzzzzz. Right by my nose. *I wonder if that's a new one that just came in*, I thought as it landed on the same little piece of potato chip in the passenger's seat.

Bzzzzzzz. Another one onto the little soda spill on the carpet in front of the seat.

Bzzzzzzz. A third. *They're all still here!* I suddenly realized in horror. *They must've all just been hiding out once the wind got too strong.*

I lowered all the windows again as I pulled onto the freeway. It was no use. I began to hear the squeaky little fly voices once again.

"Incoming! Incoming!"

"Stay close to the carpet, guys! Find yourself a crack and wedge in!"

Man, do they like my van, or what?

I went to the car wash. After that, they were finally gone. I don't know if they couldn't handle the car wash or once all the little messes were gone they had no reason to stay. I began to keep my windows up a lot more.

*   *   *

One day the following summer, we were just heading out the driveway when Anastasia, in the passenger seat, said, "Look dad, there's a fly on the windshield!" She was pointing.

I now did my best to keep the windows to the van up at night, so the fly Anastasia was pointing at was on the *outside* of the windshield, thank goodness. He was casually walking around out there, just over and in front of Anastasia and me, as we pulled out of our driveway onto 35th Avenue.[1]

I'd been driving cross-country a few nights earlier and gotten some bug splatter on the window. I mentioned this to Anastasia and said, "I bet that's a pretty tasty windshield to that

---

[1] The fly may have been a she, but Anastasia, Austen and I referred to it as "he," so that's how I refer to it here. Insect sexism, I know.

fly, loaded with slightly rotted, dried up bug guts. Bug jerky, mmm-mmm."

"*Daaa-aad.*"

Austen, who'd been playing some Nintendo game in the back seat, started chuckling. "What are you guys talking about?" he asked.

"There's a fly on the outside of the windshield," Anastasia explained, pointing. By now we were going about fifteen miles an hour, but the fly was still there, apparently having no trouble walking around and staying glued to the less-than-perfectly-clean windshield. "He apparently likes bug guts."

"Wow, that's amazing," Austen said as we pulled up to the stop sign at 45th Street, our passenger still on board.

"You know they have taste buds on their toes," I said.

"Yeah, you told us," Anastasia and Austen chorused.

"But flies don't really have toes, do they, dad?" Austen asked.

"Very good, Austen. You're right, they don't. Just little sucker feet. I should have said *taste buds on their feet*. It was an *alliteration.*"

"Hmmm," Anastasia puzzled for a second, then: "Oh, I get it! *Taste* buds on their *toes* – two ts." She chuckled.

Meanwhile, Mr. Fly – let's call him by what we were soon to learn was his proper name, Mr. *Superfly* – Mr. Superfly was still walking around on the outside of the windshield as we pulled up to the last stop sign on the way out of town. It was the same stop sign I'd pulled up to about nine months earlier, during my first encounter with Fargo flies hitching a ride. I was glad this time my hitcher was outside. What I didn't know was this particular passenger configuration was about to lead to the most remarkable experience I've ever had with a fly – thanks to my son's quick thinking.

"Wow, that's amazing," Anastasia said as we came to a stop. "He's still walking around out there." Ahead of us lay the same half-mile of paved road, nothing but fields on either side, where I'd unsuccessfully tried to lose my first Fargo fly hitchhikers nine months earlier.

"I know," I said. "The flies around here have an amazing ability to handle the wind."

"Hey, dad," Austen said. "I've got an idea. Let's see how fast we can go before he blows off."

"Okay, cool!" Anastasia said. "I'll watch the fly."

"I'll watch the speedometer," Austen said.

"You keep your eyes on the road, dad," Anastasia said.

"Okay," I agreed, and took off.

"Ten miles an hour," Austen reported.

"Still there?" I asked.

"Yep," Anastasia said.

"Twenty miles an hour," Austen announced.

"Still there!" Anastasia said.

"*Wow.*" I said. Anastasia remained silent as we approached thirty. *Could the fly still be holding onto the windshield?* I wondered.

"Thirty!" Austen announced.

"Still there!" Anastasia said, and we all started laughing.

I glanced down at the speedometer. We'd just hit thirty-five. "Anastasia, we're almost going forty, he *can't* still be there!" I said. I was suddenly sure she must be toying with the male half of the family. The fly had probably blown off back at 23 miles an hour or something.

"He is! He's *still there!*" She insisted.

"I don't believe you!" I said, laughing.

"No, dad, she's *telling the truth!*" Austen chimed in from the back seat.

"*Look*, dad," Anastasia pointed, "He's *still there!*"

I glanced at the spot on the windshield where Anastasia was pointing. *The fly was still there!* He wasn't casually walking around any more, like he had been back in Reiles Acres, when we'd only been going about fifteen miles an hour, but he was still there, hunkered down, facing into the wind.

"Oh my gosh!" I said. "He's *Superfly!*"

Austen started laughing hard. "It's a bird... it's a plane..."

I looked back down at the speedometer and started calling out: "Forty-five!"

"Still there!" Both kids were yelling now.

"Six!"

"*Still!*"

"Seven!"

The kids couldn't stop laughing as they yelled *"Still there!"*

"Eight!"

Glancing up from the speedometer, I saw we were only about a quarter-mile from County Road 20 now. I had to slow down soon, and fast – but I figured I could make it up to fifty –

"Still!"

"Forty-nine?" I said, incredulous.

"Still..."

"Fifty!"

"Awwww" Anastasia and Austen suddenly chorused, before breaking into gales of laughter.

"He's gone!" Anastasia managed to blurt out. Austen was laughing too hard to say anything.

Once again, I had to step on the brakes pretty hard to come to a stop just shy of County Road 20. Anastasia, Austen and I rolled around in our seats for a minute, laughing.

"That was awesome!!" Austen was finally able to say. "Man, that must be a good-tasting windshield you got there, dad!" Then, in a funny little fly voice, he added: "'Where'd you get dem outta town bugs, man? Dem's some good eatin'! Dat's *tasty on my tootsies!'*"

The three of us sat at the stop sign laughing for a good minute. Once again, not another car in sight. Thankful for that. You gotta love these North Dakota roads. And admire, however begrudgingly, the flies.

"That," I said, "was a *North Dakota* fly."

*   *   *

To this day, that fly reminds me of all things North Dakota. Rugged. Going about his – *or her* – business. Brave but unassuming. Weather? Hunker down. Working on something? Stick to it. Conditions less than ideal? Deal with it. Makes me think of all these great college grads that come back here every year, usually taking a huge cut in pay, so their kids can grow up in a community worthy of the term. Don't they and Superfly have more than a little in common?

*   *   *

"That was a very **Fargo fly!** " Austen said as I finally regained enough composure to pull out onto County Road 20, heading toward the freeway. We all chuckled.

"Excellent *alliteration*, Austen," I said.

"Yeah, that was amazing," Anastasia nodded, still giggling a little. I noticed she was lowering her window, grabbing her hair to keep it from flying around in the wind. "Hey, **Superfly**," she yelled out into the open prairie sky,

"How Fargo of You!"

CHAPTER 13

How Lucky We Are

The mystery of Fargo goes much deeper than these pages.

During the five years since we moved to Fargo, I've watched, along with everyone else in the world, a series of disasters unfold across our country. And along with everyone else, I've learned about the still almost completely unprosecuted malfeasance, fraud and unethical behavior that led, among other things, to the greatest financial crisis since the Great Depression and, in the Gulf of Mexico, what may turn out to be the worst environmental disaster in human history. The more I learned, the clearer it became that the primary precursor to this cascade of crises was a culture rife with unethical actions stemming from a widespread disregard for anyone else's well being – a culture that increasingly considered a self-centered, irresponsible approach to life *normal, acceptable and even, often, the* right *way to go about things.*

So I've frequently asked myself: *Can I imagine the people who live around Fargo engaging in these kinds of practices – the kinds of practices that led to these calamities – on any significant scale?* And invariably, the answer that's come echoing back has been a firm *NO!*

It turns out this isn't just the idle meanderings of my wandering mind. It's backed up by cold, hard statistics and fact.

*   *   *

This last summer of 2010, as soon as the first rough draft of *How Fargo of You* was finished, I sent it out to about a dozen of the more proven caretakers of Northern Prairie Culture. I asked each for the toughest critique he or she could give me. I knew from previous experience that the weakest parts of a rough draft, when critiqued by proven experts on a subject, can often become the strongest elements of the final work.

So of course, one of the first people I sent a rough draft of my manuscript to was the Mayor of Fargo, Dennis Walaker. I offered to take him to lunch once he finished reading it, if he would be willing to give me his honest opinion and any suggestions for improving *How Fargo of You.*

A couple of weeks later, he accepted my invitation. I met him at his office. He said he wanted to drive, which I was glad to hear, since I hadn't taken the minivan to a car wash in a long time. As we headed down to his SUV, we walked right by my vehicle, more brown dirt than white paint. "I'm glad you want to drive," I said, "because that's my dirty kid bus there."

"Well," he smiled back at me, "you must drive up and down North 45th Street all the time, living in Reiles Acres," his voice grumbled up from the bowels of the earth, the same way I was used to hearing it on television. He was referring to the mile-and-a-half of unpaved road that runs south out of our little enclave. I'd heard the mayor knew every road within a hundred miles like the back of his hand, and during the snow melt each year he liked to drive around to get a personal feel for how high the river was likely to rise. I was soon to get a glimpse, firsthand, of this kind of hands-on approach to Fargo management.

He drove us about a block, to his favorite burger joint, JL Beers. With only 24 barstools and a couple of booths, the place was packed. There were only two barstools empty, with four guys sitting between them.

"Hey guys," I said to them from behind, "would you do me a favor and scoot down one barstool to the right?" They looked over their shoulders, mouths full. They were already nodding

231

cooperatively when they caught a glimpse of the hero of Fargo towering behind me, chatting with a guy who worked at the place. Their eyes widened a bit and their butts blurred into the barstools to their right.

The burgers were great, the conversation sporadic. We were both pretty hungry and it was hard to hear in the place unless you were talking at about a half-yell.

As we finished, I remembered I was supposed to pay, and asked our server for the check. Then I reached for my wallet. My pocket was empty! I suddenly remembered I'd gotten my wallet out in the van, for some reason – and now realized, to my chagrin, I'd apparently left it on the seat.

"I just realized I left my wallet in the van," I immediately told the mayor. I started to get up. "I'll go get it so I can pay."

"Oh no," he said, motioning for me to sit back down, "I've got it." There was not the slightest hint of upset or judgment at my absent-mindedness. He just pulled his wallet out and handed our server a credit card as the check arrived. I'd asked to take the mayor to lunch and forgotten my wallet, and his only discernable reaction was a little smile, as if I'd just gotten a spot of hamburger juice on my shirt and was dabbing it with a napkin. This was notable not so much because he was the mayor, but because he was, deservedly, our most celebrated citizen. But otherwise, there wasn't anything unusual about it. I say this from experience, because, sadly, I've tested (not deliberately, mind you) a lot of people in Fargo this way. My mistakes always seem to get about the same reaction, which is to say, none at all. There's very little forgiveness around here, because so little is found that's considered worthy of taking offense at in the first place.

Still, I was stunned. It would have been the perfect time for me to say, "How Fargo of You." I didn't realize it, though, until I was just writing that last paragraph. I just watched the mayor pay and said, a little sheepishly, "Well, thank you very much."

"My pleasure, Marc." His voice grumbled up through the legs of his barstool.

We walked back out to his SUV and got in. He started to drive toward Broadway. I figured he'd turn right there, then take another right at Second Avenue, and we'd be back at his office in about a minute.

Instead, he headed west on First Avenue right past Broadway, and asked me a question. I don't remember what it was. But within a minute or two we were in the midst of a conversation I'll never forget.

"I get calls all the time now, Marc," he was soon telling me, "from reporters around the country asking why our economy here is still in good shape, asking why we never really had a recession – you know, Fargo's on the other side of the state from the oil boom, it's not like we see a lot of that money – and I just tell them, 'It's because we didn't get caught up in the subprime mess.'"

A bell went off in my head. If the mayor was right, I might be onto the biggest *How Fargo of You* story yet.

I knew a bit about the subprime mess. I'd run straight into it years earlier, before it was a mess... well, before almost anyone realized it was a mess, anyway.

*   *   *

It was early 2002. I was driving down a freeway in Phoenix, Arizona, on my way to work. On the radio, a National Public Radio business reporter was explaining that during the previous year, more adjustable rate mortgages had been sold in the U.S. than fixed rate mortgages, and the trend was increasing. She detailed how monthly payments on these mortgages would become larger – she called these "balloon payments"– a few years down the line. She explained how all these balloon payments could quickly grow even larger if interest rates started to climb.

The NPR report ended just as I pulled into the parking lot. I immediately went into the office of my boss and good friend, Rick Balfour. I worked for the company he'd started from scratch nearly ten years earlier, Nexus Multimedia. Over 90 percent of our business came from the homebuilding industry, for whom we produced high-quality 3D computer renderings of home designs. I was both the Marketing Director and Director of Client Services – I sold our services and managed the schedules to make sure our renderings got delivered on time.

We'd tripled the business since I'd arrived a little over a year earlier.

I told Rick about the report I'd just listened to. I was freaked out, and now he was too. We both knew exactly what this meant for our thriving business down the line. It was a blatantly obvious disaster in the making.

"Do you realize fixed rates are about the lowest they've been in thirty years?" Rick said to me. "And they're selling more adjustable rate loans than fixed rate loans? That's crazy!"

"And that's why the real estate market's going crazy," I said. The price of real estate had been skyrocketing and our homebuilder clients couldn't build houses fast enough – this housing boom was at least half the reason Rick's little company was booming, adding staff almost every week for a while. "They're stuffing people into houses they can't really afford over the long term – the purchasing side of the home market is being blown all out of proportion, beyond all reality of what it really is, and that's what's driving this housing boom."

Rick stated the obvious: "And a few years from now all those balloon payments are going to hit, and if interest rates have inched up a bit people won't be able to refinance and avoid those balloon payments, so the market will be flooded with foreclosures and suddenly there will be twice as many houses on the market as buyers, and we could see a crash like we've never seen before – buyers will just stay away in droves as housing prices plummet, and since almost no one buys when housing prices are dropping, it will be even worse, with even less buyers as more and more foreclosures hit the market. The price of the average house could easily drop by half."

Then I spoke the marketing coupe de gras: "And none of our homebuilding clients will be building any homes at that point, they'll have no work for us whatsoever and we'll be totally belly-up, out of business, unless we've found a totally different line of work with a totally different client base before then."

A few days later, Rick told me he'd just read a report saying that a lot of the consumer spending in the U.S. was now being fueled by the refinancing of homes – people were depleting their most basic asset, their home equity, to finance short-term purchases. I told him I'd seen or heard similar stories.

And obviously, all these refinancings were being done because a lot of people's houses were suddenly worth a lot more than they had been just a few years earlier, due to the rapid rise in real estate values across the areas of the country where the sales adjustable rate mortgages were going nuts. This sudden rise in home prices was being fueled by people purchasing homes they really couldn't afford over the long term.

The coming crash wasn't going to be just a real estate crash, we realized. It was going to be a consumer spending crash as well – perhaps even worse. But we still didn't know the half of it.

Rick and I, of course, had no idea why this was happening. That remained a mystery to us. A mystery that, over the years, as the coming crash loomed closer and closer, I became more and more immersed in investigating. What the hell was going on that we were heading for the economic cliff at an ever faster pace and no one left, right or center seemed to be noticing? And what was driving these crazy loan practices?

Eventually I got to what I believed, and still believe, to be the bottom – at least legally – of the problem. In 1999, Congress passed the Gramm-Leach-Bliley Act, named for the three Republican members of Congress who co-authored it – and it was then signed into law by the Democratic President, Bill Clinton. They all liked to call it the "Financial Modernization Act."

It eliminated the chief financial law of the land that had held us in pretty good stead for 66 years of historically unprecedented economic growth. That law was called the Glass-Steagall Act, and it was enacted in 1933, at the bottom of the Great Depression. Glass-Steagall forbid the intermingling of commercial banking, like mortgage loans, with investment banking, like start-up companies and IPOs. The best way to explain all this is probably just to recount, as best I can, a phone conversation I had a few years later with that same friend, Rick.

It was now 2008. In 2003 Nexus had merged with two other companies and I'd gone on to start my writing career. My family was now living in Fargo – and I felt like I'd finally put enough puzzle pieces together to understand what lay behind the crazy loan practices Rick and I had first become so alarmed about six years earlier. Here's roughly what I said:

"Well, Rick, I found out that after the Financial Modernization Act became law in 1999, it was no longer in the interests
of loan officers to make sure clients would be good for their
home mortgages, because the banks that sold loans no longer
had to hold on to them.

"In the old days, when a banker granted a loan, that bank
assumed the risk of that loan. So if it went bad, the banker was
on the hook. But all that changed in 1999. After they got rid of
Glass-Steagall, bankers could sell the loans they wrote as
investments to other banks or companies. So they had no
financial interest anymore in whether or not the people they
were giving loans to would be good for them.

"Are you kidding?" Rick was stunned.

"Commercial banks *used* to have to hold all the mortgages
they wrote," I continued. So any loans that went bad were a
problem for the bank. They could only make money off good
loans, loans people were paying on. But after they got rid of
Glass-Steagall, the incentives reversed. The bigger the loan a
banker wrote, the larger the fees that banker received. Then the
banker would just turn around and sell that mortgage off as an
investment to another bank or financial institution, and the
bigger that loan was, the more money the banker would make
again. So now all the financial incentives were to write the
biggest, riskiest loans they possibly could – but still make them
look like they weren't risky, of course, so they could then pass
them off as good investments.

"What a mess," Rick said.

"More than a mess. As I see it, after the Financial Modernization Act became law, small commercial bankers weren't really bankers anymore. They'd become salespeople! They had no real risk! They just had to sell stuff, and the more they sold, coming and going, the more money they made! Their job was no longer to protect the bank from bad loans and write as many good loans as possible. Instead, their new job was just to write the biggest possible mortgage for the person sitting across from them, and the bigger it was, the more fees they'd collect from the new homeowner, and then, the more they'd get for that same loan from some investment bank when they turned around and sold it to them – eliminating all their financial risk in the process!"

"How the hell did these people think this was a good idea back in 1999?" Rick asked.

"I don't know. I think they were just so full of themselves they thought they knew better than the folks who'd gotten us through the Great Depression and World War II. They thought they were smarter than the people who'd laid the foundation for the last six decades of the greatest sustained economic growth in world history, growth they were the beneficiaries of. I'll tell you one thing, though, Rick, that I learned. There was one senator who stood up on the floor of the U.S. Senate back in 1999 and fought this, and laid out almost *exactly* what would happen to United States banking practices and our economy if Glass-Steagall was eliminated."

"Who was that?" Rick asked.

"Byron Dorgan, the senior Senator from North Dakota."

*   *   *

But now, the mayor was hinting at something deeper. Something that wasn't about financial incentives and regulations. It sounded like something *Fargo*. Something *very Fargo*.

"Hmmm," was all I replied to the mayor at first, as he continued driving west on First Avenue, for how long and how far I hadn't a clue. Then I found a good starting point. "You know, one of the first things we noticed when we first looked at houses around here was that real estate prices hadn't gone crazy like they had in Arizona. Our house in Arizona at that time, it was the summer of 2005, and our house was worth nearly double what we'd paid for it just two years before. And we hadn't fixed it up at all. In fact with our dogs and kids and my less than stellar gardening it wasn't as nice as when we'd moved in. So when we looked around up here and saw houses were only appreciating at five or seven percent a year, it was a fresh breath of sanity... so you're saying that basically, the bankers up here didn't go nuts with adjustable rate mortgages like they did in Arizona and other places?"

"Yeah, that's right." His voice grumbled up from the wheel wells. *I'll have to look into this further*, I thought to myself.

For the next hour or so, the mayor drove us around Fargo. We talked about a dozen different things, our conversation interspersed with updates on whatever construction project we happened to be driving by or through at the moment – after all, it was late July, the height of *Road Construction Season*, so there were lots of sites he wanted to check the progress of, and I was just lucky enough to be along for the ride. About two o'clock or so we arrived back at the City Council Chambers, where his office is located.

"Well, Marc, I think it's a great book," he said as we got out of his SUV, "and I'll be glad to write you an endorsement. I hope it helps."

"Oh, it will," I said. "It'll help a lot, believe me. I really appreciate it."

We shook hands and said goodbye. As I got into my van, I knew without a doubt *How Fargo of You* would be a local success, at least. Our local hero – certainly my local hero – had told me he loved it.

And I suspected I might be onto the most remarkable *How Fargo of You* story yet, one that had been right in front of my eyes the entire time we'd lived here.

*   *   *

After meeting with Mayor Walaker, I sent a copy of my manuscript to Dr. Richard Rathge, Director of the North Dakota State Data Center at NDSU. A few weeks later, we had lunch just a couple of doors down from JL Beers, where I'd lunched with the mayor, at 1st and Deli. This time, I remembered to bring my wallet.

Dr. Rathge is a very congenial, athletic-looking man of about fifty. He's also a statistical expert on all things North Dakota – a veritable walking encyclopedia of data about the state. As soon as we sat down, I told him what the mayor had said to me about subprime loans.

"Well," he said, "there's a lot of problems trying to quantify the rate of subprime loans, but it's pretty clear that North Dakota has the lowest rate of those kinds of mortgages in the country."

"So a lot of the bankers here," I asked, "just continued to write the best loan for the person sitting across from them, despite all the financial incentives to do otherwise?"

"It seems that way," he nodded, smiling. "And it seems in keeping with the other things you've discerned about the culture here."

Dr. Rathge then told me that twenty years ago, when, as a postgraduate at Michigan State, he'd first been offered a job at NDSU, he'd balked. He'd never been to North Dakota, and couldn't imagine he'd find a fulfilling career here.

"So you were like me, before the first time my wife dragged me up here, huh?"

"Exactly," he said, smiling. "But then my advisor at Michigan State told me to come. 'At least it will be something on your resume,' he said to me, 'And you won't know what it's like if you never go.' So I came, and like you, I've been pretty amazed by what I found."

We then discussed North Dakota's unemployment and crime rates, also the lowest in the country. Then he told me our high school graduation rate was declining, largely due to the oil boom in the west, on the other side of the state from Fargo. "Kids can make so much money so fast, a lot of them are deciding to drop out," he explained.

"How bad is it?" I asked.

"The dropout rate in the west is up nearly sixfold," he said.

"Wow!" I said. "So what does that make it now?"

"About six percent," he answered.

I laughed. "So it was just one percent a few years ago?"

"Yes," Richard answered. "Statewide, the dropout rate is still less than three percent. I'll send you some links when I get back to the office."

Then he told me something that really surprised me. "What's not so well known is that North Dakota has the highest number of people with Associates Degrees or higher – two-year college degrees – of any state except Massachusetts. Of course, a lot of those degrees are for welding or other vocational training, skills for which there's pretty high demand in a rural state like ours. But a surprising number are for higher degrees, too."

It was one of the most informative lunches I've ever had. And over the next few days, Richard was a tremendous help sending me links via email.

One in particular stood out:

Data on subprime lending is a bit difficult and much of
what exists is not very current. The best statewide
comparison that I can find comes from the Pew Charitable
Trust. Here is their webpage
http://www.pewtrusts.org/our_work_detail.aspx?id=550

I went right to the Pew Charitable Trust website and started
digging. The numbers I found there were staggering.

North Dakota has far and away the lowest rate of expected
foreclosures in the country. While the overall rate of projected
foreclosures in the U.S. from the subprime mess is 1 out of every
33 homes, North Dakota is only projected to have a subprime
foreclosure on 1 out of every 165 homes. The second lowest rate
in the nation is 1 out of every 116 homes projected for
foreclosure in the other Dakota – also a very *Fargo* state of the
Northern Prairie – South Dakota. After that comes West
Virginia, with a much higher projected foreclosure rate of one
out of every 89 homes, then Vermont with one out of every 86
homes expected to go through foreclosure. All other 46 states
and the District of Columbia are expected to experience more
than double the North Dakota foreclosure rate. Some states, like
Arizona, where we moved from, are expected to undergo nearly
ten times the foreclosure rate of North Dakota.[5]

---

[5] It's worth noting that the next five lowest rates of expected foreclosure –
Montana, 1 out of 81, Iowa, 1 out of 79, Nebraska and Wyoming, 1 out of 64,
and Wisconsin, 1 out of 60 – are all, to some extent, connected to what I refer

But what this really says about Northern Prairie Culture is being completely lost on the rest of the country.

*   *   *

The national articles and news stories the mayor told me he was being interviewed for began to come out this last summer. In July, Newsweek did a feature titled *The Great Great Plains,* calling Fargo and Omaha "the nation's new boomtowns." CNN spent a day up here taking a similar tack. And there have been plenty of others, all saying pretty much the same thing.

And they've all completely missed the point.

All these stories and articles are about *stuff.* See how well these folks doing with their *stuff* while the rest of the country is having so many problems with their *stuff.* "Boomtowns." "Oil and Energy." "Money." "Employment." And on and on and on.

But the entire reason we're not in the kind of trouble the rest of the nation is in is because the vast majority of people around here value *relationships* over *stuff.* How else do you explain

---

to as Northern Prairie Culture.   The rate of foreclosure in northern Minnesota, away from the Twin Cities – from what little evidence I've been able to glean, which isn't much – also appears to be relatively low. But if any evidence points to Fargo lying at the heart of this culture, it's the statistics associated with the subprime mess. Except for South Dakota, North Dakota is so different in degree from the rest of the nation as to be, arguably, different in kind.

bankers foregoing easy profits, and instead, continuing to write loans that, by and large, were appropriate to the person sitting across from them? Our bankers did right by their neighbors and customers – and thereby themselves, their families and the world. Commissions and profits – *stuff* – be damned.

So it turns out *How Fargo of You* isn't just a bunch of cute stories. Okay, some of them *are* cute. And they are stories. But at its heart, ***How Fargo of You*** is about a fairly high-tech, well-educated community in the early 21st Century where the vast majority of people are, amazingly, a lot more concerned about nurturing relationships than acquiring stuff. And this nurturing is largely anonymous. As these pages illustrate over and over, people here work to build great relationships with everyone around them, not just people they know well enough to decide they're worthy of the effort. Our bankers are just one case in point. Our tens of thousands of sandbagging volunteers – the vast majority of whom weren't working their butts off to save their own property, but rather, that of others, almost always people they didn't know – are another. And every other story in this book is a testament to this underlying reality.

The reason we're not having trouble with our *stuff* is because we haven't been foregoing or neglecting our relationships in pursuit of *stuff*. In fact, it's quite the opposite – every experience I've related in this book, and lots of others I haven't, involves foregoing stuff or convenience in favor of building or nurturing relationships.

But the most visible result of this to outsiders, paradoxically, is that North Dakotans aren't having a lot of trouble with our *stuff* while everyone else is. So the trouble with the recent spate of news stories and articles, complimentary as they are, is they all completely miss the point. They're all about *stuff*. There's no way, for instance, that anyone reading any of these national news articles could get the first clue as to why my executive cab driver and his family moved back to Fargo.

They sure didn't do it for *stuff*.

*   *   *

My knowledge ends there. Why North Dakota and, to a lesser extent, almost every place from Iowa and Nebraska up through Manitoba, Alberta and Saskatchewan have low crime and unemployment rates, high graduation rates, and a lot of stories to tell like those in these pages is still largely a mystery to me. I like to speculate about the Homestead Act – perhaps the greatest example in human history of giving people who were willing to work the means with which to support themselves; I like to speculate about the agrarian basis of the local culture, which Jefferson and other genius observers of history believed to lie at the heart of every healthy phase of civilization; I like to speculate about the climate – which forces people to think ahead or die, and view nature with respect and humility; and I like to

247

speculate about the beliefs of the people here. But there are other areas of our country just as homesteaded, just as agrarian, with similar beliefs and the same hard winters and soft summers, that can only dream of having a culture as healthy as the one we enjoy here. Perhaps it's some combination of these ingredients, and lots of others I've yet to learn about, coming together in just the right amounts, stirred in at just the right moments, like a great recipe, that made it all happen.

I've got one thing to say to the mystery chef.

How Fargo of You.

CHAPTER 14

What Fargo Really Means

Maybe there's hope for us humans.

I don't want to get all anthropological on you – this book is, after all, centered around the heart, not the head – but the undeniable truth is, *these stories are important.* I don't mean my personal stories. I mean the millions of stories like them, that anyone who's spent any time here can offer up as soon as they're asked.

These stories aren't just heartwarming and funny. They're much more than that. I want to tell you why I think so.

Ideals are important. They drive and affect a lot of human behavior. Crazy Utopian ideals – especially those closely tied to racism or some other unbending ideology, like the ideals that drove Nazi Germany or the Soviet Union (which were almost opposite ideals, by the way) have probably caused more death and destruction than any other intellectual force in history. Healthy ideals, on the other hand, based on achievable realities – like the ideals outlined in the works of Locke, Montesquieu and others, leading to the ideals first made famous in the United States' Declaration of Independence, which have been spreading around the world ever since – these kinds of plausible ideals have arguably produced more positive changes in the way human beings interact with each other than any other intellectual constructs ever created.

So ideals are worth thinking about very seriously. I believe there are three important questions to ask of any ideal anyone proposes. First, "Is this ideal plausible?" Second, "If so, would it do anyone any good if it were achieved?" And third, "Who would be harmed by achieving this ideal?" And the sad truth is, most ideals ever envisioned by human beings flunk at least one of those three simple questions, usually more than one. Ideals are usually pretty simple, and usually pretty wrong. Coming up with an ideal that *really is ideal* is an extremely difficult thing for us to do.

Before I first visited Fargo, the only times I'd ever come across visions of the kind of community I've found here was in: a) fiction (*Shangri La*, for instance), b) personal stories from extremely rural pioneer communities of the past (*Little House on the Prairie* or ancestral stories I'd heard from fourth or fifth generation Arizonans, that kind of thing), or c) Utopian treatises (either political, religious or economic, these always seem premised on the idea, "If everyone just thought the way we do, and understood what we understand, then we could run things the way we know they should be run and everything would be so wonderful!" – and *at least* one of these "ideals" always seems to be lurking behind *every* devastating human conflict or genocide).

Those of us who live within what I've chosen to refer to in these pages as *Northern Prairie Culture* – however many tens of thousands of square miles that culture actually encompasses – can honestly report that, here in the first part of the 21st Century, a place like ours isn't just some cockeyed screwball dream, it actually *exists*. This may be even more important than I think it is. And I think it's pretty darned important.

Because my five years here have taught me it isn't about being married to some way of thinking or some belief system. It's about taking care of each other *without* thinking too much. It's about paying a lot more attention to caring behavior than to other things, all of which, I've concluded from living here, are mere trifles by comparison.

Besides a safe, sane place for my kids to grow up in, the most important thing Fargo has given me is hope for humanity, and the future. If it can happen here, it can happen. It's not impossible.

And the only thing that comes close to expressing my gratitude to everyone within at least a couple hundred miles of where I sit as I type the final words of this final chapter is...

How Fargo of You.

And as far as I'm concerned,
there's no greater compliment in the world.

Let's Do This Again

Taking down names, handing out smiles:
Contribute your own story to **How Fargo of You, Too!**

There are many, *many* reasons a book titled *How Fargo of You* should hold more than my singular reflections as a newcomer to Fargo. I want to tell you the three I think are most important.

First, it's more fun. Fargo – and as you know, by *Fargo*, I'm referring to something common to most everyone within at least a couple hundred miles of here – is a shared experience. And it's a lot more fun to have stories going around the campfire, rather than listening to the same storyteller drone on all night.

Second, the truth is *How Fargo of You* is not my story – I just have a tiny little piece of it. It's a much larger, ongoing story that my family and I, primarily through the intelligent efforts of my wife Charlene, have happily entered. I have the advantage of seeing things that happen here in stark relief against the backdrop of the first fifty years of my life, lived in other places – places where *How Fargo of You* kinds of things just didn't happen. This gives me a unique perspective, from which these stories almost tell themselves. So I've used that perspective to get this started.

But whenever I tell a *How Fargo of You* story to someone from around here, a look of recognition quickly sweeps across his or her face. And right then and there, I get to hear some remarkable *How Fargo of You* story from that person's life. Everyone who's ever been within a few hundred miles of this town has some of their own *How Fargo of You* stories. These stories aren't unique to me. But from this book, people in other areas of the country could get the erroneous impression there was something special about me, that made all these wild things happen. That's not it. This stuff just happens around here. All the time. To everyone this side of a total grump.

This is an important point. Fargo has a lot of successful, home-grown businesses and businesspeople. Many of them travel a lot, because they're good enough at what they do that big companies in the urban centers of the country pay them

LET'S DO THIS AGAIN

pretty well to fly in on a regular basis. And, inevitably, the question comes: "Why are you in *Fargo?*" – with the word *Fargo* usually sort of sneered out.

So our Fargoan emissaries gallantly try to explain. But it's not that easy. Trying to get Fargo across to someone who lives in a big city is like trying to describe homemade pie from the Hunter Cafe to someone who's only tasted the pre-packaged stuff sold at convenience stores. And besides, Fargoans aren't prone to bragging. So we fumble around with some small answer like, "Well, the schools are great and I have a lot of family nearby," or something like that, and the eyes of our urban associates sort of glaze over. They think we're crazy, because obviously we could make so much more money if we just lived in Los Angeles or Houston or wherever – and they have no idea of the much greater value we get by living here. All in all, these inquiries are usually disheartening. We should change that.

So in the next year or two I want to put together *How Fargo of You, Too!*, loaded up with lots of great stories from lots of great people around here. It will pack a wallop. So whenever one of our business travelers hears, "Why are you in *Fargo?*" she or he can just hand the questioner a copy of the book and say, "Here, this'll give you an idea," and try not to be too smug. I hope it's hard.

So if you have a favorite *How Fargo of You* story you'd like to tell, please email it to stories@howfargo.com. Don't worry if you're not the world's best writer. Just tell the story. If we publish it, we'll polish it up as needed – with your approval, of course. And you'll get a little piece of the next book, too.

Finally, from the first time the words *How Fargo of You* jumped out of some hidden recess in my brain (a recess that knows just the right thing to say, and which my wife wishes I would access a lot more often), it began to occur to me that *How Fargo of You* was something we all could have a lot of fun saying to each other around here.

Too often, we take the best things in life for granted. Ten or twenty years later, we realize those things have faded away through neglect. Only then, looking back in longing, do we fully appreciate what we had. I never want that to happen to Fargo. What we have here is truly priceless – you can't buy it, at any price. It's a culture most human beings who have ever walked the earth couldn't imagine lay within the possibilities of human nature. I certainly didn't, before suddenly finding myself amidst a whole bunch of the most self-reliant and, simultaneously, most generous people I've ever known.

I hope *How Fargo of You* catches on, so that someday in the not-too-distant future, whenever someone does something great for someone around here, they'll hear choruses of, "Oh! *How Fargo of You!*" In my dreamy little head, I imagine these four words helping us take more notice of all the wonderful things people do for each other around our little piece of paradise. I imagine it helping us acknowledge and take even greater responsibility for this wondrous culture we're part of, so that maybe twenty years from now, we'll be even more *Fargo* than we are today, rather than looking back with longing on what used to be. And I'm betting that one way to make that happen is by inviting everyone to contribute their own *How Fargo of You* stories to a second book.

I could easily fill another book with more *How Fargo of You* stories all by myself. But among the many things the great people of the Fargo area have taught me is this: More hands not only make the work go faster, they can make it a lot better and a lot more fun... *Especially* when those hands belong to the wonderful people behind one of the best kept secrets in the world: The amazingly warm culture of the Northern Prairie.

One last thing. The next time you see or hear about someone around here doing something above and beyond the call of self-interest, something that makes your life or your family's life or our community's life richer, please tell them, for all of us:

How Fargo of You!

Twelve Reasons to Come to Fargo, Twice as Many Not to

Everything you should know about Fargo before coming. Or not.

Twelve Reasons to Come to Fargo

1. **For a visit.** This is the best reason to come, no matter your other reasons. Experience Fargo for yourself, and make up your own mind. That's the only way to discover how you

react to Northern Prairie Culture – and, as I explain in the next list, *Twice as Many Not to*, how it reacts to you.

2. **For your kids.** This is why we moved here after our first couple of visits. We'd learned enough to know this region would be a much better place for our kids to become young adults than any other we knew of – but we had no idea *how* much better. We discovered that by living here. Don't call the moving company just yet, however. Read the rest of this list and the one that follows before packin' up and headin' for Fargo with the kids.

3. **You're a highly qualified, skilled worker in a technical field and have a good job offer from a firm in the Fargo region.** We have a high-tech sector that's growing like crazy. Working for tech companies here – where Microsoft, for instance, has their second-largest field campus on the planet after Silicon Valley – will only help you along in your career. And you'll get to experience the wonders of Fargo without a cut in pay, unlike so many others who come…

4. **You're willing to take a cut in pay and do jobs well beneath your highest skill set to be a part of this community.** This assumes you've visited enough to make this kind of judgment. Demographic studies show that about half the people who grow up here and move away after they graduate from college do exactly this – they move back, taking a sizeable cut in pay, when they begin to raise families. See Chapter Nine, *A Very Fargo Cab Ride* (a ride I

received from a recently returned young executive and father). So Fargo is loaded with overqualified, underpaid talent. You have probably never experienced a job market like this in your life. So it's your call. If you recognize this is what you're heading into, want do it anyway, and have prepared for it intelligently, you should fit right in. Because one of the main reasons to come to Fargo is...

5. **You value people and relationships and doing right by the other person over stuff and money and doing whatever you can to acquire as much as you can for yourself as quickly as possible – and you're willing to forgo some income to live in a community where that's the prevailing attitude about the way life ought to be lived.** This goes very deep and has tremendous implications. It's a major reason why North Dakota has a much healthier economy than any other state in the country as I write this. Bankers and mortgage brokers sold far fewer adjustable rate loans here than their counterparts in other states, at least partly because they valued doing right by the person sitting across from them over their own personal income for that month. So North Dakota has only a fraction of the foreclosures most other states have. As a result, our real estate values have risen while most other states' have crashed, and we haven't experienced the myriad of negative repercussions those crashes precipitate. So when you read articles about how well the North Dakota economy is doing, recognize it's

largely because most people here put relationships first, money second – and that, oddly enough, is a big reason we don't have any significant money problems! Kind of ironic, huh? Even the irony around here is pretty cool. See Chapter Thirteen, *How Lucky We Are*, for details.

6. **You prefer simplicity to complexity, patience to pushiness, perseverance to squirreliness, engagement to aloofness, honesty to distrust, gratitude to indifference, courage to sneakiness, kindness to selfishness and a lot of other good stuff over a lot of other seemingly expedient approaches because you recognize in yourself a basic preference for things measured only by the heart over things measured with ledgers, scales and tape measures.** Hey, that's pretty good.

7. **You're really tired of a status-driven approach to life, from financial one-upmanship to the narcissistic, show-off-as-much-as-ostentatiously-possible consumerism that has spread across much of our country over the last half-dozen decades or so.** In other places I've lived, lots of people drove Mercedes or BMWs or something else they really couldn't afford, putting themselves in a position where they were likely to do questionable business deals or not spend enough time with their kids, just to make sure they had enough to make their next car payment. Around here, there are lots of people who can afford a Mercedes, because they've never bought a car that cost more than cash on hand, so all that

payment money has been saved over the years. But despite the fact that so many here could easily afford an expensive car, almost no one owns one. Unless it's a Mercedes or a Cadillac SUV, because those are actually kind of practical in these parts. This is to say nothing of the tens of thousands of McMansions across the country being foreclosed on as I write this. By contrast, I was visiting with a friend in a middle-class neighborhood in North Fargo recently, and she was telling me who her neighbors were: a leading surgeon; a professor emeritus; a woman who recently sold her business for seven figures, and others with similar resumes I don't recall – all still living in the same houses they've lived in for decades, because they've developed deep relationships with their neighbors and the immediate community, and they like it there. Why would they move? To prove that they're better than their neighbors? That's the last thing they'd want to do, and even if they did, they're smart enough to know that might involve moving to India and doing charity work, not moving into a fancier house. Not that people here never move. But when they do, they do it for a more substantive reason than acquiring a fancier place that shows off better.

8. **You like being constantly reminded by Mother Nature you're not in charge and enjoy the challenge of having to continuously think ahead to avoid calamities that can cost lots of money or, better yet, life and limb!** I spent most of my life in the desert, where people who aren't properly

prepared frequently die from exposure... after three days or more. Around here, about 45 minutes of ill-prepared exposure can do the trick. In the desert, a fairly flimsy house will do just fine. Around Fargo, only a well-built house properly prepared in the fall will survive the winter without pipes breaking and other ruinous results. Getting out the other side of winter is sometimes even more trying, involving sandbagging to save the entire community. Heck, not paying attention to how you're walking for a second or two can land you on your back between November and April. Anything less than pretty good intelligence rigorously and responsibly applied won't get you through a year around these parts. I'm sure this has more than a little to do with why Northern Prairie Culture is the way it is.

9. **You understand the tale of the Tortoise and the Hare.** Things have to get done right around here or you might as well not do them, from repairing a freeway to walking the dog. The most obvious side effect of this is people seem to move a little more slowly and deliberately in this part of the world, whether working, driving or just having a cup of coffee. But don't be fooled by the apparent ho-hum pace of people around these parts. World-class companies who set up offices here often find they need far less personnel – sometimes *only half* the number they anticipated – to handle a given workload (see Introduction, *How Fargo of You Stories*).

10. **You're in search of the most overqualified, underpaid, competent and ethical work force in the United States.** I've explained this already (items 4-9 above). For more details, read the whole darned book. If you're not from around here, you'll be amazed.

11. **You like thinking up ways to stun others with unexpected kindness, or taking impromptu advantage of sudden opportunities to do so.** The earlier items on this list don't really touch on this, but it's the central point of the whole book. The phrase *How Fargo of You* came out of my search for an adequate response to the regular onslaught of over-the-top help that people hand out like lollypops around here. I've concluded this is probably the central game in this culture. Most cultures seem to have a central game going on, just under the surface, which you can catch onto if you hang around long enough to connect the dots. When I lived in L.A. in the '80s, for instance (as a twenty-something musician toying with making it, it seemed the place to be), the central game appeared to me: How narcissistic can you be? Can you be more narcissistic than the next person? Can you prove through superficial means – baubles or Mercedes or McMansions or gorgeous boyfriends or girlfriends (sometimes both) or fake boobs or whatever – that you love yourself more than others love themselves? Of course, that game doesn't really work, because the harder you push your narcissism, the more narcissistic you become, and the more

narcissistic you become, the more shallow you get, and the more shallow you get, the more, deep down, you actually start to hate yourself. But here in the Northern Prairie, there's a very different central game, one that goes something like: Can you stun, even overwhelm, others with unexpected acts of kindness or just plain decency, especially anonymously? These are not really random acts. They seem to arise out of a steady state of readiness, and occur whenever the opportunity arises. Unlike the cultural game I observed in L.A., this one pays tremendous dividends to everyone involved, generating an upward cultural spiral rather than a downward one.

12. **You like to pump before you pay.** 'Nuf said. (See Chapter One, *Our First Visit.*)

Alright, that's *Twelve Reasons to Come to Fargo.* Now here's:

Twice as Many Not to

1. **You Require Warm Weather.** If so, the best you can do around here is stay inside six months out of the year with the thermostat cranked up or do the snowbird thing and head south for the winter. A lot of older folks who no longer have kids in school do the latter. Somebody a while back told me he had a 60-something year-old uncle in North Dakota

who'd developed really bad arthritis and could hardly get around – until he moved to Arizona, where it almost completely disappeared! He suddenly started playing 18 holes of golf five days a week! So some people really do, apparently, require warm weather.

2. **You Want to Meet Someone Who Looks, Sounds or Acts Like Any of the People in the Movie** *Fargo*. Some people insist these kinds of characters exist – but I've lived here more than six years now, done a bit of traveling around North Dakota and Minnesota, and have yet to meet one. I suppose I can imagine there's a Marge Gunderson out there somewhere, a pregnant, heroic sheriff who's totally ho-hum about her heroism – I recognize her steady, methodical approach to the challenge of the day, whatever it happens to be, as *very* Fargo – but I have yet to meet anyone who wears an overly exaggerated, several-generations-old Swedish accent "as a badge of honor," the way Frances McDormand, who won a well-deserved Academy Award as Best Actress in that role, described her character as doing. As far as I've been able to see by living here for more than half a decade, the overly drawn characters in the movie *Fargo* are really caricatures who only exist in the make-believe world of that movie, which, as moviemakers Joel and Ethan Cohen have been telling people for years, was *not* based on a true story – they only put "THIS IS A TRUE STORY" at the beginning of their film, they insist, to make their over-the-top characters

and situations seem more believable. See the first page of *Notes on the Chapters*, following this list, for details.

3. **You Think You Might Be Able to Take Advantage of Us Because We're Such Nice Folks.** There's a cultural immune system around here. People who don't act very Fargo aren't treated very Fargo. And bad guys are so few and far between they stand out – I mean, they might as well be wearing pink pajamas. They get nabbed amazingly fast. See items 4-7 below, and Chapter Seven, *The News from Fargo*, for more details.

4. **You're Arrogant, Rude or Just Naturally Defensive – or You Want to Test the People Around Here to See if We're Really as Nice as *How Fargo of You* Might Lead You to Believe.** Over the last eighteen months or so, I've talked to every Fargo newcomer like myself that I could find – people of all colors and backgrounds, from all parts of the country; many from other parts of the world. I wanted to know if my experience was unique. One pattern has emerged with amazing consistency: If you "get" Northern Prairie Culture and behave in a friendly, non-aloof manner around here, hold doors open for people, smile and say "hi" to strangers, thank the folks who are holding the door for you, drive courteously and so on, you will have the same kinds of experiences I've had – and it won't matter what color you are or how funny your accent is. On the other hand, if you come into town and act like a New Yorker yelling at fellow New

Yorkers in New York, you'll just get blank stares... and those stares will leave you a lot colder than another New Yorker yelling back at you (which in New York is almost a sign of affection, I know – but that's a different book). I've talked with folks the color of Michael Jordan who "got" Fargo right away, and they've consistently had the same kinds of experiences I've had. Conversely, I've talked with folks as white as Wonder Bread who decided that when people asked them "Where are you from?" it was some kind of veiled criticism, a slight aimed at their accent, and they responded defensively. To them Fargoans seem stand-offish, and probably are, because they are, taking offense at one of the more common questions asked of almost every new acquaintance around here, intended as a friendly gesture. I've come to think of this "get" Fargo or "don't get" Fargo phenomena as our cultural immune system. If someone "gets" Northern Prairie Culture enough to participate, they're welcomed into it immediately, almost everywhere they go. If they don't, they're not. And with a culture as wondrous as this one, isn't an immune system a good thing to have? Makes me wonder if this immune system – making people who catch onto the "above and beyond the call of kindness" ethic feel fabulously welcome, while making people who, for whatever reason, don't feel welcome feel even less welcome – makes me wonder if this instinctive reaction, both good and bad, isn't a significant factor in deciding the mix of people who stay in the region... and the mix of people who leave.

5. **You Think Fargo is as White as Wonder Bread and Find That Appealing.** It's not. According to Madison Elementary School near downtown Fargo, more than fifty dialects are spoken among the thousand-or-so students on campus. You will see garb from various countries worn in the city. NDSU has some of the best science- and math-related departments in the world, and many East Asians, Indians and Pakistanis have come to work and study here – and incidentally, seem to get along just fine in North Dakota. We also have thousands of residents from war-torn countries – the local non-profit Lutheran Social Services has been rescuing folks from Bosnia, Somalia, Sudan and other areas for over a decade, bringing them to the Northern Prairie. How this very humanitarian work will eventually play out, for everyone concerned – there's a huge gap between the demolished cultures most of these people come from and the Northern Prairie Culture and its immune system – remains to be seen.

6. **You Like Lots of Cultural Diversity.** When I lived in L.A., the way people treated each other in East L.A. was totally different from the way people treated each other in Korea town, which was totally different from how people behaved in West Hollywood. We don't have that kind of deep cultural diversity here. On an average day in Fargo, you'll

see clothes and styles from several continents, and skin colors of every shade. You'll hear accents from around the world. But it seems, to me, at least, that most of the people here have adopted the prevailing Northern Prairie approach to interpersonal relations. Doesn't matter what their ethnic background is. For instance, I go to one Chinese restaurant where most of the staff are clearly first-generation Americans, speaking broken English, but they treat me with the kind of friendly kindness I've come to expect in the Northern Prairie. It's a very busy, successful place. There was another one in town, where I actually preferred the food, but the staff, mostly Anglo, often weren't that friendly. Don't ask me why, I haven't a clue – aloof isn't normal around here. As a result, the place was usually pretty dead, despite the great food. And now it's gone. So I'm not talking about accoutrements of culture like food or clothing or furnishings, which are very diverse in Fargo, or about ethnic background or race, which we also have a wide range of – I'm talking about actual day-to-day culture. Around here, if it's Northern Prairie Culture, it usually does pretty well, and if it looks or acts or feels like something else, it tends to get the immune system treatment.

7. **You Think You Might Get Away With a Crime Here.** You won't. Crimes are few and far between around these parts. So police have lots of time to become very well trained, and they stay well rested. When a real crime finally happens

they salivate at the chance to put all that good training and rest to work staying up late catching bad guys. Furthermore, citizens help the police to an extent that keeps bad guys from getting any rest. So they don't get a rest until they get arrested! See Chapter Seven, *The News From Fargo*, for more details.

8. **You Think Everyone Should Always Be in a Hurry For Everything.** We're not in much of a hurry around here, unless the river's rising. This often bothers people who like a big-city pace. See item 9 on the previous list, *Twelve Reasons to Come to Fargo*, for more details.

9. **You Don't Like Talking About the Weather.** Last winter, on a very snowy, wind-swept evening, our neighbor to the west called from her job, where she was working late, to ask if I could still see her house across the street. It wasn't a silly question. In whiteout conditions, I sometimes can't. That night, I could just barely make it out. She had to decide whether to try to make it home that night. According to the news there were already about forty occupied vehicles stranded in various locations around the county that the sheriff's office was trying to locate in order to rescue the occupants (How did people get rescued before cell phones, I wonder?) So our neighbor wisely decided to stay at the Radisson downtown, and her employer covered it. So, yeah, we talk about the weather. A lot.

10. **You Don't Like Nature Continually Reminding You Who's In Charge.** Around here, you'll be reminded. Regularly. Lots of reminders. Ignore them at your own risk. Arrogance can be a death sentence around here.

11. **You Don't Like Danger, Hard Work, Thinking Ahead, Self-Reliance or Helping Others.** Should be self-evident by now that any such dislikes would disqualify you for a happy life anywhere within a few hundred miles of Fargo.

12. **You feel the need to register as a Democrat, Republican or member of some other political party.** North Dakota is the only state in the nation where citizens don't need to register to vote. So you can't. All you can do is show you're an American citizen living in North Dakota. Then you vote. What a concept! See Chapter Six, *North Dakota Politics: An Oxymoron?*

13. **You Think the Proletariat Should Rise Up and Throw Off the Shackles of Capitalism.** Pretty much everyone around here embraces a free-market economy. It works really well when a higher standard than just making money – a standard of "the only reason to do business is to provide a product or service other people really need, and provide it really well at a good price and in a way that is as helpful as possible" – is wholeheartedly embraced by the whole culture, as it is here.

14. **You Think Anything Labeled "Socialism" Must Be Bad.** North Dakota has the only state-owned bank in the country.

We're also the only state outlawing agribusiness – all farms must be family-owned. These and other measures often labeled "socialist" really help us prosper and do right by each other and the country as a whole. So we embrace them. Our thoughts and decisions are not dictated by political labels of any stripe – just by what's right and will do the most good for the most people as best we can see it at the time.

15. **You're on Welfare.** Not a lot of help for you here. A little, perhaps, for a little while, possibly, but only if you've worked here for a longer while. So definitely a reason not to come. And about six months out of the year, if you're not well-clothed and well-sheltered around these parts, it's a lot worse than no fun at all.

16. **You Have a Business Idea that Could Be Highly Profitable In the Short Term But Which Lacks Redeeming Social Value and Might Be Destructive Over the Long Term.** Say, for instance, you want to sell a lot of adjustable rate loans to people who won't be able to afford them once interest rates rise, so they'll probably be foreclosed on at some point in the future. But this will be extremely profitable for you before then, because in addition to the fees you'll collect for selling these mortgages, you'll then use these mortgages to create a lot of faulty "investment packages" to sell around the world, leaving you with no risk on the inevitable future defaults. This might work out splendidly for you in much of the rest

of the country, where you might find lots of people willing to sell these mortgages and investment packages, and they'll find lots of people to buy them – whether out of greed or ignorance or desperation or some combination thereof. But in North Dakota you'll be almost completely out of luck. You won't find many people to sell these mortgages and they'll find even fewer to buy them. See Chapter 13, *How Lucky We Are*, for details.

17. **You Like Complexity.** Financial derivatives. Deceptive packaging. Ridiculous combinations of over- and under-regulation, often of the same market. Drug ads that work by describing all the ways you can get sick and die through the proper use of a product (even Orwell would be amazed!) Internet overload. On and on. The world is going complexity crazy. The general consensus seems to be, "Oh, well. Can't be helped." As if we can't really control the complexities we ourselves create. Not around here. One of the reasons North Dakota stayed further away from the subprime mess than any other state, I believe, is a general distrust of things that are overly complex: The more parts there are, the more things there are to go wrong; the more interdependent all those parts are, the greater the chances just one failure will cause a cascade of failures through the whole system… so let's just keep things as simple as possible. That's a *Fargo* approach. There's a reason nature has no trees with a million branches, beehives with a billion

bees or planets with highly oscillating orbits: Too much complexity leads, inevitably, to chaos – so anything that gets too complex soon ceases to exist in its current form. There seems to be an instinctive understanding of the dangers of too much complexity rooted deeply in Northern Prairie Culture. Better yet, there seems to be an inherent sense of urgency to curtail it early on, before it gets too unwieldy. Best of all, people around here are pretty dogged and competent at finding ways to keep things as simple as possible. So if you like all the over-complexities the modern world is plopping out like candies onto a conveyor belt on *I Love Lucy*, you won't like it here. We eschew complexity. That's just my rough stab at what seems to be a very prevalent attitude that lies deep in the heart of Northern Prairie Culture. Don't ask me why. It's not like everyone around here enjoys studying Complexity Theory in their spare time like I do. It probably stems from lessons learned over generations of farming the land, where science, after all, got its start – a heritage most people around here are still connected to, but much of the modern world has lost touch with. Just a guess.

18. **You Have a Great Resume, and Since North Dakota Has the Lowest Unemployment Rate in the Country, You Think You Can Just Show Up and Get a Job that Pays Pretty Much Whatever You've Been Making.** Our low unemployment rate is just the blade of grass growing out of the clump of dirt

sitting atop the tip of the iceberg of our very unique job market. Imagine a place where people with extremely high standards want to raise their families, so lots of them move there (or back there). You could end up with a place that held twice as much talent per capita as other places. The laws of supply and demand being what they are, the talent in that area would only be worth half as much as in other areas, given the same demand for talent. That, roughly, is why I think the job market in Fargo is what it is – an employer's paradise. See Chapter Nine, *A Very Fargo Cab Ride*, for details.

19. **You Don't Want to Take Vitamin D Every Day at Least Six Months Out of the Year.** You should, up here. No kidding. Not a lot of sun exposure October 15 through April 15. Your body needs that D! So unless you eat reindeer or fish all winter long like a Viking or an Eskimo, take your pill. Or drops. *Take 'em!*

20. **You Want to Convert People to a Particular Religious Doctrine.** Haven't had a knock on my door from someone trying to sell a particular belief system the six years we've been here. Used to get half a dozen a year in Arizona and California. Little wonder. People are happy here, they treat each other with the Golden Rule or well beyond – and most seem to know what they believe. That's a tough sell.

21. **You're into Status or Think Stuff and Money are More Important than People and Relationships or...** See item 7 on the list preceding this one, *Twelve Reasons to Come to Fargo*.

22. **You think SUVs are the bane of Mankind.** There are a lot of them around here. Al Gore wouldn't like it. But I don't think anyone's come up with anything nearly as good at moving people and stuff around the Northern Prairie regardless of conditions. Not yet.

23. **You Want to Negotiate Your Infidelity.** As soon as I heard about this one – the idea that couples ought to "negotiate their infidelity" – I knew I had to include it on this list. It's a near-perfect illustration of how the rest of the world often looks to us as we watch it from up here. Last summer, an erstwhile Australian escort with the stage name "Holly Hill" released a book titled "Sugarbabe" about her search for a sugar daddy. Despite the fact that both her resume and book make it abundantly clear exactly what she is (hint: *not* a scholar), world media instantly glommed onto her brilliant suggestion that women ought to "negotiate infidelity" with their partners, because "cheating men are normal," and "men are hard wired to betray women on [sic] the long term." Practically overnight, everyone from CNN to Fox to CBS was falling all over themselves to interview this woman as if she had just developed a new Theory of Relativity or something... which, in a way, I guess she had, but I'm guessing it's not one Einstein would consider worth fussing

over. Anyway, by the fall, Dr. Phil and others in the eight-figures-a-year-television-therapy racket were all talking "negotiated infidelity" ad nauseum. In California, this could be a very serious subject – because just about every married person in that state, of any level of attractiveness or complete lack thereof, would probably need more than just his or her fingers and toes to count all the people he or she knew who might want to help them participate in a little infidelity. (This isn't pure conjecture; I lived there, both north and south, over a period of years – but that's another book.) But up here, *no*. Aside from "negotiated infidelity" being complicated, it's just way too unkind a concept for most to even consider here. Too much letting the base instincts run roughshod over our better angels. We prefer our better angels trampling our base instincts, *Thank You*. And if you can think ahead more than just a few inches (let me apologize for that phrase right now) you can see that negotiating infidelity is like trying to climb straight up a ninety degree snowbank – a thrilling snowmobile ride for a second or two, perhaps, but then it's really going to hurt. For a while. Maybe forever. So if you want to negotiate your infidelity, don't come to Fargo – because, chances are, even if you're pretty good looking and a smooth talker, you might never find anyone to practice any infidelity with… and if you were to look too hard, I wouldn't be surprised if you discovered some painful aspects of the Northern Prairie

Cultural Immune System with which I have had the honor of not becoming acquainted.

24. You Like to Pay Before You Pump.

There's you go. You are forewarned.

Which only leaves one thing left to say…

How Fargo of Me!

Notes on the Chapters

First page of the book: Lowest unemployment rates by state from the Federal Bureau of Labor Statistics website (A map will show you every state listed here is a Northern Prairie state except Wyoming, the eastern half of which is Northern Prairie.)

2008: North Dakota, South Dakota and Wyoming tied for lowest unemployment rate in the nation at 3.1%; Nebraska second lowest at 3.2%. (See http://www.bls.gov/lau/lastrk08.htm)

2009: North Dakota has the lowest unemployment rate in the nation at 4.5%; Nebraska 4.8%, South Dakota 5% and Iowa fourth lowest at 5.6%. (See http://www.bls.gov/lau/lastrk09.htm)

2010: North Dakota still lowest at 3.9 %; Nebraska still second at 4.7 %, South Dakota still third at 4.8% and Iowa still fourth lowest at 6.1 percent. (See http://www.bls.gov/lau/lastrk10.htm)

2011: Last month available as this book goes to press is September, with North Dakota reported at 3.5%, Nebraska again second lowest at 4.2%, and South Dakota again third at 4.6%. (See http://www.bls.gov/web/laus/laumstrk.htm for latest figures)

Preface to the Third Edition

1) On October 7, 2011 (just before this Third Edition went to press) the U.S. Bureau of Labor Statistics reported the national unemployment rate for September was 9.1% (see http://www.bls.gov/news.release/empsit.nr0.htm)
2) North Dakota unemployment rate for September 2011 was 3.5%, the lowest in the nation (see notes above)
3) All other statistics mentioned in the Preface are discussed in detail in the later chapters of the book and the notes on those chapters.

4) The best place to hear what the Coen brothers have to say about the movie *Fargo* is in the Special Features section of the Special Edition DVD of the movie (which is the only *Fargo* DVD available these days, I believe). The one point they continue to insist on is that some people around here actually talk the way their characters do in the movie. Having been here a little over half a decade, traveled around a bit, and not yet found one person with anything remotely as sing-songy as the accents that movie is populated with, I simply don't believe them. They are, as their "THIS IS A TRUE STORY" opening to the movie *Fargo* illustrates, major leg pullers. Big time. Just because they've admitted they made the whole story of the movie up doesn't mean they must now be telling the truth about the way people talk. They're still pulling. Maybe they found one little town somewhere in the far north backwoods of Minnesota and took all the cast there to listen to them, saying "This is how we need you to sound, because everyone around here talks like this." But I haven't found that little town yet, or run across anyone from it.

Introduction

1) My funny storytelling singer-songwriter friend is still busy playing, singing and writing, and his full name is Skip Eaton. You can learn more about him at: www.skipeaton.com

2) All the brief *How Fargo of You* stories in the Introduction are described in greater detail later in the book, except for this one:

The "former mayor" was Bruce Furness, who was kind enough to read the first draft of my manuscript a few months before it went to press. Then Bruce and I had lunch. The story about Cargill was one of the many fascinating stories Bruce told me. He also told me that baseball great Maury Wills, on his first visit to Fargo, had an identical experience to the one I describe in Chapter One, and had pretty much the same reaction I had.

Chapter 2

1) On the next page is a chart that represents one kind of information Charlene and I were going on in 2005 when we decided to move from Arizona to North Dakota. As you can see, in 2001 North Dakota had the second highest graduation rate in the nation, while Arizona had the second lowest (along with Washington DC and Florida).

Since 2001, good data on high school graduation rates have become much harder to find, because many states are now employing deceptive practices. On page 285 I've included a link to an excellent article from the *New York Times* about this.

Civic Report November 2001

High School Graduation Rates in the United States

Alabama	62%	Montana	83%
Alaska	67	Nebraska	85
Arizona	59	Nevada	58
Arkansas	72	New Hampshire	71
California	68	New Jersey	75
Colorado	68	New Mexico	65
Connecticut	75	New York	70
Delaware	73	North Carolina	63
District of Columbia	59	North Dakota	88
Florida	59	Ohio	77
Georgia	54	Oklahoma	74
Hawaii	69	Oregon	67
Idaho	78	Pennsylvania	82
Illinois	78	Rhode Island	72
Indiana	74	South Carolina	62
Iowa	93	South Dakota	80
Kansas	76	Tennessee	60
Kentucky	71	Texas	67
Louisiana	69	Utah	81
Maine	78	Vermont	84
Maryland	75	Virginia	74
Massachusetts	75	Washington	70
Michigan	75	West Virginia	82
Minnesota	82	Wisconsin	85
Mississippi	62	Wyoming	81
Missouri	75		

This table shows high school graduation rates throughout the United States for 2001, excerpted from a report prepared by the Manhattan Institute for Policy Research, *High School Graduation*

Rates in the United States, which you can read online at these two links:

www.manhattan-institute.org/html/cr_baeo_t1.htm
and
http://www.manhattan-institute.org/html/cr_baeo.htm.

Data on high school drop out rates around the country are now much harder to decipher than in 2001, because the incentives built into *No Child Left Behind* have induced many states to start using tricks to obscure their actual dropout rates. You can read about this for hours if you Google "high school dropout rates." There's one good article from the *New York Times* about what's going on that was published a couple of years ago titled **States Data Obscure How Few Finish High School**. It can be found at:

www.nytimes.com/2008/03/20/education/20graduation.html

2) Microsoft Fargo is the company's second-largest field campus. With over a thousand team members, it is surpassed in size only by their Silicon Valley field office. They cite the high work ethic, trustworthiness and education level of the Fargo area workforce as three of the many reasons they chose to base some of their most important operations here.

Also see Microsoft press releases such as:
http://www.microsoft.com/presspass/press/2007/may07/05-22MSFargoExpansionPR.mspx
and
http://www.microsoft.com/presspass/features/2002/apr02/04-24greatplains.mspx

and North Dakota Governor John Hoeven's 2009 State of the
State address (page 9):
http://www.denalicompanies.com/pdf/hoeven.pdf

And there are also some interesting blogs:
http://content.techrepublic.com.com/2346-1035_11-158886.html?cbsi_footer_menu=
and
http://blogs.techrepublic.com.com/tech-news/?p=1020
and
http://microsoftjobsblog.com/blog/silicon-valley-seattle-fargo/

Chapter 6

1) The 2006 debate I heard on Prairie Public radio was
   between Roger Johnson, a Democrat who had held the
   office of Agriculture Commissioner since 1996 and who
   was re-elected in 2006, and Doug Goehring, a Republican
   who was later appointed North Dakota Agriculture
   Commissioner by Governor Hoeven in 2009 when Roger
   Johnson resigned to become President of the National
   Farmer's Union.

2) Here's a North Dakota state website that describes the state's status as the only state not requiring voter registration: http://www.nd.gov/sos/forms/pdf/votereg.pdf

A brief excerpt from that site:

North Dakota....The Only State
Without Voter Registration
No Voter Registration

North Dakota is the only state without voter registration. There are several states that register voters on Election Day, which is known as same-day registration.

Although North Dakota was one of the first states to adopt voter registration prior to the turn of the century, it abolished it in 1951. It is also worth noting that North Dakota law still provides cities with the ability to register voters for city elections. However, only one city registers its voters for city elections – Medora - a small city located in southwestern North Dakota.

North Dakota is a rural state and its communities maintain close ties and networks. North Dakota's system of voting, and lack of voter registration, is rooted in its rural character by providing small precincts. Establishing relatively small precincts is intended to ensure that election boards know the voters who come to the polls to vote on Election Day and can easily detect those who should not be voting in the precinct. This network of small precincts reduces the need for voter registration.

Chapter 7

1) You can do all the simple crime research I describe in Chapter 5 by scrolling down on these websites until you get to the table showing crime statistics and rates per 100,000:

Here's a website detailing Fargo crime statistics:
http://www.city-data.com/city/Fargo-North-Dakota.html

Here's a website detailing Phoenix crime statistics:
http://www.city-data.com/crime/crime-Phoenix-Arizona.html

Here's a website detailing Glendale, AZ crime statistics:
http://www.city-data.com/city/Glendale-Arizona.html

Using the numbers from those three websites:

The number of murders per 100,000 population in Fargo, 2001-2004: 2001: 0; 2002: 0; 2003: 0; 2004: 1.1. Average (1.1 ÷ 4) .275 murders per 100,000 per year. (If you crunch the numbers on this website in detail going off of Fargo's population, this average is even a little lower, .273 murders per 100,000 in population between 2001 and 2004.)

The number of murders per 100,000 population in Phoenix and Glendale, AZ combined: 13.5 (Arrived at by adding Phoenix and Glendale's 2001-2004 murder totals (895), dividing by 4 years = 223.5 average number of murders per year, then taking Phoenix and Glendale's combined highest population (2004: just slightly over 1,650,000) and dividing by 100,000 =16.5)
Then dividing 223.5 by 16.5 = 13.545 murders per 100,000 per year

And 13.545 ÷ .273 = 49, ergo Fargo's murder rate is 1/49th that of the Phoenix/Glendale area.

Chapter 8

1) Normally the word cafe is spelled with an accent over the e – café. But the dictionary indicates it can also be spelled without the accent, simply cafe. Since that's the way Deb and her family have chosen to spell it on their card, sign and other materials, that's how I have spelled it in my story about them. I'll just add that it's not surprising they would spell it without the accent. It's simpler and less pretentious, while still remaining within the bounds of accepted usage. You can't get much more Fargo – or *Hunter* – than that.

Chapter 9

1) Kim Kelsey is a Registered Architect and a LEED Accredited Professional who was named "North Dakota Young Architect of the Year" in 2007.

2) When Joan reviewed this chapter, she told me that Lee Massey, the president of Media Productions, who I'd described as "a young looking forty-something," was just about to celebrate his 60th birthday. Stunned would be an understatement. I refused to change the text of the chapter, however, since it describes exactly how he looks to me. Instead, I'm just adding this note.

3) If you're not from around here, you've probably wondered if Minnesota's official slogan, "Land of 10,000 Lakes" is hype. Well, no, it isn't. In fact, it's typical

Northern Prairie understatement. Ottertail County, about an hour east of Fargo, has more than 10,000 lakes all by itself, if you count all the small ones right after the snow melts in the spring! Granted, some are pretty small, a couple hundred feet across and just five or six feet deep. But that's the heart of the "lakes country" Kevin was referring to.

Minnesota's website says that the state has "...11,842 lakes that are 10 acres or more. Depending on one's definition of a lake, we have seen numbers as high as 15,000." You can read this and lots more at:

http://www.netstate.com/states/intro/mn_intro.htm

Chapter 10

1) After I sent Tom this chapter to review, he told me he was only six-foot-two. Since I don't normally overestimate people's size, I'm convinced it's Tom's powerful build – he's not overweight, but he reminds me of the trunk of a decent-sized oak – anyway, I think it's his build that makes him look huge to me.

Chapter 13

1) Anyone who's not familiar with the long series of cut corners that led to the 2010 Gulf oil disaster – each corner

cut placing the savings a few dollars at greater importance than the well-being of the entire Gulf of Mexico and all the people living along its coasts – must never watch the news… which is okay, I don't blame you. As for all the similarly irresponsible conduct and unethical actions leading to the greatest financial crisis since the Great Depression, there are at least a dozen extremely well-researched, meticulously documented, highly readable books at this point, from the hyper-bestselling *The Big Short* by Michael Lewis to *A Colossal Failure of Common Sense* by Lawrence G. MacDonald to *It Takes a Pillage* by Nomi Prins. But the easiest, fastest way to get the full picture of what led to our recent brush with complete financial collapse, which still continues, every day, to put more hard working, well-educated people in homeless shelters across the country – is to watch the widely acclaimed documentary by Charles Ferguson, *Inside Job*. It will blow your mind – and, by comparison, make the peaceful isle of Northern Prairie Culture this book celebrates that much more impressive, by giving a frighteningly clear picture of the sea of chaotic greed and malfeasance, from the top down, that surrounds our tranquil refuge of sanity here.

Recent legislation hasn't fixed the banking incentive problem that arose out of eliminating Glass-Steagall. It's just added layers of bureaucracy and policing. This appears to be what the big banks preferred (they protesteth too loudly Wall Street Reform). Any talk of reinstituting Glass-Steagall gets shrieks of horror and million-dollar PR attacks out of Wall Street, since the profit centers of most big banks have now shifted toward

all sorts of squirrely financial activities that became possible once Glass-Steagall was eliminated. The best one-hour talk I know of on this is a spellbinder from former IMF Senior Economist Simon Johnson, now a Professor at MIT, which he gave on October 21, 2011. Simon's talk is exceedingly well hidden on C-Span 2's website on that date under the nondescript "2010 Financial Regulations" and preceded by a 50-minute talk by Sheila Blair... but here's the link:
http://www.c-spanvideo.org/program/FinancialRegulationsLaw
After you go here, first hit the play arrow, then move the slider ahead to minute 49, when Professor Johnson is introduced. Then sit back for a truly mind-blowing hour of plain-spoken economic reality.

2) I was wrong when I told my friend Rick that Byron Dorgan was the "Senior Senator from North Dakota" in 1999. He was our Junior Senator. For the speech he gave when stood before the U.S. Senate and laid out what would happen if the Financial Modernization Act was passed into law, eliminating Glass-Steagall, I recommend his 2009 book *Reckless!*

3) After the First Edition of **How Fargo of You** went to press, but before it had come out, I happened to end up in a room with a few of Fargo's leading bankers. I couldn't resist. I told them about Chapter 13, and my ideas about why North Dakota almost completely avoided the subprime banking mess. In typical Fargo fashion, they didn't want to take credit for our good fortune – they gave most of the credit to their customers. "Nobody around here wanted an adjustable rate loan," they told me. "They just wanted fixed-rate loans. And

those were more profitable for us, so that's what we sold."

"In other areas of the country," I enjoined them, "people who couldn't possibly have qualified for a fixed-rate loan were having adjustable rate loans shoved down their throats hand-over-fist. I was getting calls, everyone I knew was getting alls, homeless people were getting calls all the time trying to sell us adjustable rate mortgages. I'm not exaggerating. So if all you were selling here in North Dakota were fixed-rate loans, that means almost no one here was trying to sell mortgages to people that would get them into trouble, mortgages that everyone would be better off without, mortgages that bankers and brokers in other parts of the country couldn't sell enough of."

Well, yeah, you're right, they admitted, *of course we didn't do **that***. And that's how I managed to get a few of the leading bankers in Fargo to take just a little credit for our good fortune here.

How Fargo of them.

Marc de Celle's previous work includes the acclaimed 2004 report *Anticipating Crisis*. Warning of accelerating risks to U.S. infrastructure well before these dangers were widely recognized, *Anticipating Crisis* garnered accolades from leading scientists, authors and experts across a wide range of fields. Marc lives with his wife, Charlene, and their two children just outside of Fargo. *How Fargo of You* is his first book.